FATHER ROBERT J. KUS

DREAMS
FOR THE
VINEYARD

JOURNAL OF A PARISH PRIEST — 2002

RED LANTERN PRESS
WILMINGTON, NORTH CAROLINA

Dedication

To my folks
Robert T. & Mary Jean Kus
of Stow, Ohio

Acknowledgments

My greatest thanks go to the parishioners of St. Catherine of Siena Parish who entered my life and captured my heart during my years with them.

Special thanks also go to Pat Marriott, Nolan Heath and Allen Sanderson of St. Mary Parish in Wilmington, N.C. who helped with the editing and design of this book.

Special thanks also go to the fine folks of CreateSpace who helped bring this book to life.

Introduction

The purpose of this book is to provide a glimpse into the daily life of a parish priest in the early part of the 21st Century in North Carolina.

A secondary purpose of this book is to add to the rich history of the Parish of St. Catherine of Siena in Wake Forest, N.C. and the Diocese of Raleigh of which the parish is part.

This journal is a personal reflection of just one priest, so in no way should it be seen as an official mouthpiece for other priests, the parish as a whole, or the Diocese of Raleigh. Further, I remind the reader that this journal is a one-year "snapshot" of my life. Hopefully, the person who wrote this in 2002 is not the same person who lives today.

Father Robert J. Kus
Wilmington, N.C.
October 2013

MARCH 2002

March 13, 2002 – Wednesday
Wake Forest, N.C.
52 F – Rainy

This afternoon, I gave a pep talk at the Velvet Cloak to certain priests of the Diocese of Raleigh who are about to engage in the God's Work: Our Challenge campaign. Because St. Catherine's and I were so successful as a pilot parish, I've been chosen as the "pep talk guy" for pastors and pastoral administrators. St. Catherine's raised $2.1 million while our goal was $1.3 million.

On the way home from the Velvet Cloak, I was listening to National Public Radio. It had a program talking about diaries and journals. Journaling has been something I have wanted to do for some time, but I have just been lazy. As a writer, I need to develop more discipline. Thus, on this rainy afternoon, I begin what I hope to be a long and rich experience of journal writing.

I just received two books in the mail: *Wounded Prophet: A Portrait of Henri J.M. Nouwen* by Michael Ford, and *A Whole New Life* by Reynolds Price. I'm looking forward to reading the life of Nouwen, one of my favorite spiritual writers. The other book is for my sister Jeanette who battled cancer and is in remission. It's an autobiography of a Duke University professor of English who suffered from cancer and won his battle. Because I'm on the verge of being approved as an Adjunct Associate Professor in the Duke University School of Nursing, I want to support Duke things.

This evening, I go to St. Andrew's in Apex, N.C. for Lenten Reconciliation Service. So much for my usual day off. Not that I'm complaining! I love being a priest and wouldn't trade it for anything in the world!

March 14, 2002 – Thursday
Wake Forest, N.C.
70 F – Partly sunny

Last evening, at the St. Andrew Lenten Reconciliation Service, Fr. Dave Brockman told me that the Priest Council has given its approval for priests to live alone. Further, we may build duplex-type rectories just as I have designed for St. Catherine's. I'm thrilled at the news. Living with someone else is draining. Building a relationship is work. I don't need to work at church and then come home to work again. I get my energy from solitude and spend it with people. So, now I have to get some advice as to whether the parish should simply buy the house I'm in or another house, or build a duplex house. Bob Neal, a parishioner, has offered to build a rectory at cost.

Fr. Des Keenan is celebrating the 10:30 a.m. Mass this Sunday, and he will then hear Confessions all through the 12:30 p.m. Mass in Spanish. That will be wonderful for the Hispanics, as I don't follow what they're saying in Spanish. Plus, if they have something to discuss with a priest, they will have that opportunity.

March 20, 2002 – Wednesday
Wake Forest, N.C.
70 F - cloudy

I just finished celebrating Mass at the dining room table. I love Wednesday, my day off, for I can celebrate Mass by myself and take plenty of time to talk with the Lord. It's so peaceful not having to be "on" as a presider of a group.

This evening, I will be going to St. Michael the Archangel parish in Cary, N.C. (my ordination place) to celebrate the Sacrament of Reconciliation. It will be my last Lenten Reconciliation Service this year. Though I dearly love celebrating the sacraments, I am getting a bit tired going out so many evenings.

Because my parish is so very young demographically, it's unusual that we have funerals. However, I had one on Saturday (Jerry "Mr. Z" Zimmer

Sr.) and one on Monday (Imogene "Imy" Griesedieck). Both came from wonderful families.

On Monday evening, I went to The Forks Cafeteria here in Wake Forest to meet with Dr. Tom Jackson, Pastor of Wake Forest Baptist Church, and others to discuss chemical dependency and how we can help. It is an interesting group. I think I'll continue to go. I'm not sure how I can help. Though chemical dependency is one of my main areas of specialization in sociology and nursing, there is only so much time I can devote to things outside my parish.

I'm looking forward to a visit on Friday from Jim Weetenkamp, a man I graduated from high school with in 1961. We were at Maryknoll Junior Seminary together in Clarks Summit, Pennsylvania. Our seminary was nicknamed "The Venard" after Saint Theophane Venard, a French martyr. Jim never became a priest and has been working in business all these years. I'm anxious to catch up on his life. I find it so very fascinating how lives unfold! I am extremely grateful that my life is turning out so well. I feel that I'm on my fifth lifetime! Talk about an interesting and fulfilling life! On the other hand, I feel I'm just warming up and the best is yet to come! Jim contacted me from seeing me on the Internet on a website called Classmates.com.

March 21, 2002
Wake Forest, N.C.
60 F – Partly Sunny

The Reconciliation Service at St. Michael's went for one hour and 50 minutes! We definitely did not have enough priests to celebrate the sacrament. I was glad to finally get finished. Thankfully, I was one of the few priests who got to sit down during the sacrament.

On the other hand, I always love to go to St. Michael's, as that is where I was ordained almost four years ago and it is where I celebrated my First Mass of Thanksgiving. It is hard to believe that it has been four years already! On the other hand, with all that has happened in my priesthood so far, it seems I have been a priest much longer.

I'm looking forward to doing a presentation this evening on The Eucharist (Mass plus Communion) for the parents of students who are making their First Communion this spring. We'll have about 89 Anglo kids making their First Communion, plus 12 Hispanics. We'll do these First Holy Communions in several groups at various Masses. What a joyful thing it is to celebrate First Holy Communion!

Fr. Dave Brockman from St. Luke's told me last evening that they're dropping their Confirmation age group down to 8th grade. I asked him how they were then able to keep the teens continuing faith development during high school if they already had their Confirmation. (It is a theory that Confirmation is the "carrot" that keeps youth coming to Faith Formation classes, and if it weren't for that carrot, the youth would never come to youth groups.) Dave said that the students who are being confirmed don't want to come for Confirmation training sessions that last for an hour and a half and then stay for another hour and a half on top of that for youth group. Their theory is that if a parish has a decent youth group, the kids will continue to come. Now there is an idea worth looking into!

Fr. Dan Oshwald, who was ordained with me, told us last evening about his recent trip to Kingston, Jamaica with young adults. Msgr. Mike Shugrue, Vicar for Priests, is planning on going to Uganda this summer. It is good our guys are getting foreign land experience as it makes us all more Catholic in our vision. My own travels to Central America, Mexico, South America, Uganda and Europe have made me appreciate my land so much more and become more detached from the things of this world. We Americans are so very spoiled!

March 22, 2002 – Friday
Wake Forest, N.C.
43 F – Sunny

It is a little after 3:00 in the afternoon. An arctic blast has touched our land today, but it should only last for the day.

I just finished reading John Shekleton's *A Jesuit Tale* (Danbury, CT: Rutledge Books, 2000). I thoroughly enjoyed reading this novel, but then I usually like books with priest heroes. What a wonderful thing to give the world—a fine novel. I hope that someday I, too, can put together at least one novel.

As I write this, I'm waiting for Jim Weetenkamp to come for our reunion. What fun it will be catching up on the 41 years that have passed since our high school graduation!

March 23, 2002 – Saturday
Wake Forest, N.C.
Sunny – 58 F

What a wonderful experience it was to have Jim Weetenkamp visit me! I would never have recognized him after 41 years.

We had dinner at Lucky 32 restaurant in Raleigh and talked of old times at The Venard and how our lives have unfolded. Jim has crafted a wonderful life for himself. He has worked at CSX Railroad since 1964 – the year he left Maryknoll College Seminary. He hopes to be able to retire in a couple of years and then build his dream home in Jacksonville, Fl. where he lives with his significant other. Jim has turned out to be such a wonderful person, comfortable in his skin and at peace with the world. How terrific!

Jim says that when he read my email at work, in which I told him the highlights of my life, he yelled a cheer when he reached the end part where I told of my ordination as a priest.

We tried to call our former classmate Bob Rafferty, but I didn't have the phone number and couldn't get it from the Stow, Ohio operator. Oh, well.

Jim left this morning for Virginia where he will meet with his family and friends. I think his visit has given me a renewed commitment to be more faithful to my writing goals as I realize how quickly life passes by. If we are not careful, we can waste it so easily, and we cannot turn back the hands of time to do it over again – we each only get one chance!

I'm very glad that it is sunny and warmer today, for this evening, we begin celebrating Palm Sunday. Because we meet outside for the blessing of the palms, a rainy day would be a drag!

March 24, 2002 – Passion (Palm) Sunday
Wake Forest, N.C.
Sunny – 60 F

When I first became a priest a couple of years ago, I had a very bad Palm Sunday experience. At every Mass, something went wrong—a missing Lectionary, trouble with the sound system, people who weren't prepared to read their part in the Passion, and the like. Ever since that experience, I have had the impression that Palm Sunday (as most people call it), was my unlucky liturgical day.

Well, it seems I was right. In my first Mass, my battery went dead, and the third Mass wasn't great shakes either. At the first Mass, I had to actually stop the reading of the Passion because a small child wouldn't stop crying, and the mother seemed to be oblivious to the commotion the continuous crying was causing the community. I asked her to please take out the child, as it was in distress. I hope she understands, but who knows. Some people don't have any sensitivity to the behavior of their children. I don't mind kids who begin to fuss. After all, with 1,400 children and youth in my parish, that is expected. It is when the parent lets the child cry continuously in the main sanctuary that it becomes problematic.

Fortunately, the 10:30 a.m. Mass went well. It was for Frankie and Bobby Senn, relatives of mine. Little Frankie and Bobby Stout, twins who sat in the front row, got a big kick out of me saying the names "Frankie and Bobby."

Now that the Hispanic community is taking charge of putting the collection money into the safe by themselves, I am able to greet the people as they come out of church. I'm feeling much closer to the community, and vice versa. I love the Hispanic community very much and am delighted to see it growing. I think that within one year, we may have an overflow group watching Mass in the cafeteria by closed circuit TV as the 10:30 a.m. Mass crowd does now. What a great "problem" to have!

March 27, 2002 – Wednesday
Wake Forest, N.C.
60s F – Partly sunny

Yesterday, we had a great Chrism Mass. The bishop gave one of his best homilies, ever. It was good to see the priests once again. Naturally, I sat next to my friend Mark J. Betti during the Mass. That is our tradition. Not only are we both from Cleveland, but we match in size. Plus, we very much enjoy each other's company. The speaker we had for the pre-Chrism Mass workshop spoke about the Gospel of John. Though he's an expert in his field, his presentation was pretty dry.

During the Chrism Mass, we had a terrific thunderstorm, and it was still pouring down on my way home. Fortunately, I made it home okay and was most grateful to go to bed.

The parish has been very busy as always, and I feel I'm getting irritable at times. I think most of the problem is worrying about the finances and all the building that I have to do in the future. Then, on top of everything, working with the diocese is sometimes less than great. Just the other day, for example, a diocesan official called to say we never got permission to pave our lower parking lot. We are expanding it and putting in an egress onto W. Holding Ave., but now we won't be able to pave it until we get permission from the diocese—which could take about six months. First, we must have our self-study done, followed by a site development plan by an architect, and then approval from the Diocese of Raleigh Building and Real Estate Commission. It's incredible that we get anything done, but that's bureaucracy for you!

Though today is my day off, I went to visit the Pre-K 3-year old class. They made me a banner with the Stations of the Cross painted on it, and they sang "Happy Birthday." We had our photos taken together. It's great to be wanted!

March 30, 2002 – Holy Saturday
Wake Forest, N.C.
74 F – Partly cloudy

As I write this, it's almost 11:00 p.m. and I need to get up at 5:30 in the morning to begin my day. I can't believe I'm 59 years old today! My spirit is very young. It is only the body that is older. Time flies quickly, yet in another sense, I feel as though I've had at least five lives already! I think that is because I have done so many things in my life and been to so many places. I must say that my life has been incredibly full and very, very interesting. And to think that I'm just warming up!

My heart is filled with joy and gratitude to God on this special night. I have just come from church where we celebrated the Easter Vigil. Thankfully, it went well and we brought 16 into the Catholic Church this evening. Tomorrow, I have three more baptisms at the Mass in Spanish. God is truly blessing my ministry and St. Catherine of Siena Catholic Church. The whole congregation sang "Happy Birthday" to me at the end of the liturgy!

As I reflect on my life this evening, I am able to identify certain threads that continually run through it. The first is my love for Jesus Christ and His Catholic Church. No matter where my travels have taken me, I have always had the Church as my anchor. Prayer has always been a foundation. That is why it sounds so bizarre to me when someone says, "I forgot to pray" or, "I don't have time to pray." To me that's like saying, "I forgot to breathe today" or, "I didn't have time to breathe." Chatting with God takes so little time when you come to think of it. We can do it while walking, listening, driving, bathing or whatever.

Another thread in my life is the love of helping others. Despite the fact that I love solitude and get my energy in solitude, I find I've always had jobs that deal with people in an intimate way. My adult life has basically been all about nursing in hospitals and teaching in universities. Because I was in a Big Ten University (Iowa), and because it is a "publish-or-perish" institution, I had to write. Eventually, I found that being a writer was an integral part of my identity just as much as R.N. and university professor. Now, I am a parish priest, the greatest joy of all. Each of these professions is designed to enter into people's lives and help them in their life journeys.

Another thread is my sense of optimism and excitement about being alive. The world is such an incredible place to me. There are not enough hours in a day to do all the things I want to do. Adventure lurks just around the corner. No matter how dark it becomes, the sun is just waiting to come out smiling. How a person can be bored on this planet is a complete mystery to me!

Well, that is it for this birthday. I hope that I have many more and that I can grow in holiness and serve the Lord better and better each day. God, help me be a great priest and a great saint. That is all I ask of you.

March 31, 2002 – Easter Sunday
Wake Forest, N.C.
Cloudy in the morning, with thunderstorms and flash floods in the evening

It's Easter Sunday evening as I write this. What a glorious day this was! We estimate that we had about 3,000 people for Easter Vigil and Easter Masses. We gave away car license tags with the old St. Catherine of Siena logo, and they went like hotcakes. I'm glad we had plenty for the Hispanic community to take.

Many people stopped to say how much they enjoyed the homily. I talked about the butterfly as nature's symbol of the Resurrection. Just as the caterpillar is not supposed to remain a caterpillar, but to turn into a butterfly, we also need to advance in our life journey. We need to die as our old selves and be reborn into new selves – selves with the triple love ethic of Jesus Christ as our center. I also invited people who have drifted from the Church to come back.

Soul Purpose, our Praise & Worship Band, played at the 10:30 a.m. Mass. They obviously had practiced and were wonderful.

In the Mass in Spanish, we had the baptisms of three babies. The community sang "Happy Birthday" to me and gave me gifts of spiritual bouquets, a shirt and money. After the Mass, the community took over our kitchen and dining room for a Mexican dinner to sell food for the Hispanic retreat on April 13th. After Mass, I told two couples that I would come to bless their homes on Wednesday. I also told the Hispanic community that though my Spanish is limited, the love I have in my heart for them is great. I truly do love this community!

The only bad thing this Easter Day was news that my friend, Fr. R., was relieved of his active ministry duties because of accusations that he hurt someone in 1967, 35 years ago! I can't help wondering how many good and holy priests will be ruined by false accusations or mistakes made when they were barely out of their teens. That is why I believe that priests today definitely need to practice what I have termed "Defensive Ministry."

APRIL 2002

April 1, 2002 – Easter Monday
Wake Forest, N.C.
65 F – Sunny with fluffy clouds

What a beautiful day it is today! There were about 18 for Mass this morning. Thankfully, the office is closed for the day. I was amazed at how good the place looked considering we had 3,000 people for services this weekend! The Hispanic community left the kitchen and dining room in excellent condition.

I mowed the lawn earlier for the first time this season. Don, our custodian, put fertilizer on it, so I'm hoping that it will be one of the best lawns on the block. Soon, I'll plant impatiens by the front door, as they do so very well there.

The workers are at the church building the new Trinity Center— which is what we're calling the new four-room classroom building.

Right now, I'm waiting for Mom and Dad to arrive from Ocean Isle Beach, N.C. where they have spent February and March. They will head back home to Uniontown, Ohio on Wednesday morning. It will be nice to see them again and catch up on things.

I'm continuing to read Fr. Andrew M. Greeley's *Letters to a Loving God: A Prayer Journal*. I'm halfway done with it and am enjoying it very much. I like the simplicity of his writing. I'm also impressed at how much he accomplishes in his life despite what seems to be constant self-doubts, fatigue, colds and over-extendedness. I can't help but wonder if a person who is not famous, like myself, could get a major publisher to publish a prayer journal should I write one. Or are his prayer journals published simply because he is Andrew M. Greeley?

April 6, 2002 – Saturday
Wake Forest, N.C.
55 F – Sunny

I had a wonderful visit with my folks. They came from Ocean Isle Beach on Monday and left on Wednesday morning for Ohio. While they were here, we swung by St. Raphael's and visited St. Francis of Assisi parish, both in Raleigh. I wanted them to see the size of our parishes here—huge. That's what I'm faced with building for St. Catherine's, which will someday be a huge parish, God willing.

This week has been a hectic one. Not only have there been many things to occupy my time, but also many of the concerns have been very "heavy." For example, one of our parishioners has started volunteering at the Tri-Area Ministry. It appears that volunteers, at least on Tuesdays and Thursdays, have been taking food for themselves instead of giving it all to the poor. There are also complaints that donors are treated rudely because the volunteers have to get up and sort the things the donors bring. I have also heard complaints that many of the poor, especially the Hispanics, are treated "like dirt."

Yesterday, I got a letter from a neighbor on Tyler Run complaining about the construction of the Trinity Center and how it is affecting her property. I called her up and told her that she had never contacted me, but that I would be delighted to visit with her. I also told her that the current mountain of dirt will be leveled off, so that what exists now is merely temporary.

The world continues to spin crazily. The current sex scandal in the Catholic Church continues to make news, and the Israeli army is doing all it can to harm the Palestinian people. I pray for peace in the Middle East, and I look forward to the day when there will be a free and independent Palestinian state. Maybe then we can have peace.

A reporter from the Q Section of the *News & Observer* interviewed me the other day about the current sex scandals in the American Church. Who knows what she will print. I sent her a copy of my "Defensive Ministry" article that I wrote in 1997 while still a seminarian at St. Meinrad. I told her that any priest can give his opinions on the current sex scandal situation, but I can offer a new slant: How priests can protect themselves from false accusations. I will try to get the *National Catholic Reporter* on Monday to look at the article. It is incredibly timely right now. I think with all the publicity about priests and pedophilia, there will be a heightened suspicion of priests, making them more and more vulnerable to false accusations of improper behavior. Thus, it is imperative for all priests in ministry to practice what I call "Defensive Ministry."

This weekend, I'm preaching on the gift of the Sacrament of Reconciliation and likening it to the Magic Castle. Only people who recognize that they are lost can see the Magic Castle, a place filled with riches that are theirs for the taking. Likewise, only those who take advantage of the Sacrament of Reconciliation can receive its many graces—graces such as reconciliation to God and the Christian community, a sense of wholeness, freedom from sin and more courage for the journey.

The latest edition of the *NC Catholics* came yesterday, and there on the front page was a photo of my friend, Fr. Mark J. Betti and myself at the gathering at St. Francis of Assisi for the Chrism Mass.

April 7, 2002 – 2nd Sunday of Easter
Wake Forest, N.C.
Partly sunny – High 50s F

Last evening, when I got home from the 5:00 p.m. Mass, I received a call from Fr. Jerry Sherba from the Cathedral. He told me he had just anointed one of my parishioners, Brian M. at WakeMed.

I immediately went to WakeMed and visited with Brian's wife in the second floor waiting area. It turns out Brian is only 45 years old, and he had a massive stroke today. Early in the day, he mowed the lawn and this afternoon coached his son's soccer team. When he came home, he went in the bathroom with a severe headache. When he didn't come out of the bathroom, his family went in and found him unconscious. Brian has five children and a wife, Denise. Brian is an assistant principal at a middle school in Granville County, and his wife teaches pre-school at Hope Lutheran. Their five kids are active in our Faith Development program. I offered the 10:30 a.m. Mass for Brian and his family.

The liturgies this weekend went very smoothly. Many people have not yet come back from spring break, so there were extra chairs at all the Masses. A group of Searchers came to celebrate the 10:30 a.m. Mass with us, and I asked them to stand up and be recognized.

The Q Section of today's *News & Observer* had the anticipated special report on the sexual scandal in the Catholic Church. Bishop Gossman and Fr. Mike Clay, vocation director, were interviewed and quoted extensively.

I was one of the small "quotables" along with the Rev. Larry Campbell of Faith Baptist Church in Zebulon and Katie Mundell, a senior at Leesville High School. My quote was:

> "Some people think this is a gay thing. It's not. One year ago, the church in Africa was having a major scandal of priests abusing women [...] I'm hypersensitive to 'Defensive Ministry', [which] is conducting a ministry in such a way as to minimize the risk of false accusations or misrepresentations of what you're doing. We should protect ourselves, today especially because people are so hypersensitive, it's possible to misrepresent." – The Rev. Bob Kus of Wake Forest, Pastor of St. Catherine of Siena

So, there you have it. It's always interesting to see what a reporter will take out of a conversation. This wasn't bad, actually.

I'm thinking that I'll contact the *National Catholic Reporter* tomorrow to see if they are interested in doing something with my article on "Defensive Ministry." Now, more than ever, it is important for priests to practice their ministry in a way to minimize false accusations or misrepresentations.

April 8, 2002 – Monday
Wake Forest, N.C.
70 F – Sunny

Last night, I watched *October Sky* on TV. I had seen it before, but it was just as good the second time. It's about a teenager from Coaltown, West Virginia who developed a great love for outer space. He very much wanted to escape the life of a coalminer like his dad, but he faced many obstacles. Fortunately, with the help of three of his classmates and some adults, he won first place in the national science fair with his rocket. Eventually, he went on to become a rocket scientist with NASA.

I love stories of people who follow their dreams and are able to accomplish them! I hope that I can write such stories someday. Much of my preaching, I find, is how we can do almost anything with God's help.

Today, I called one of the editors of the *National Catholic Reporter* and told him about my "Defensive Ministry" article. He asked me to send it and the whole special edition of *The Priest* to Kansas City, Mo. via overnight FedEx. Perhaps he can use it and, hopefully, it will help priests to be more careful in their ministry.

This afternoon, I met with Bob Neal, who has offered to build me a rectory at cost. We looked at a property that would be great for a house, but we're not sure the parish owns it. I'll have to explore that further.

April 9, 2002 – Tuesday
Wake Forest, N.C.
70 F – Cloudy

I had lunch this afternoon at The Healing Place, an alcohol treatment center for homeless men in Wake County. I was invited as part of a group of clergy. I like the good work the center is doing because it has a strong Alcoholics Anonymous base and because many of the head people are AA persons. I didn't get much out of my visit, however, because they talked about issues I already know about. Having done most of my research and writing in the area of sobriety among gay American men of Alcoholics Anonymous, I found the presentation not too informative.

This afternoon, Gael, our Business manager, found that we own the property on which Bob Neal and I would like to build the rectory. That is good news, although we still have to get approval from the city and the Diocese of Raleigh.

April 10, 2002 – Wednesday
Wake Forest, N.C.
Light rain – Partly cloudy – High 60s F

As I write this, it is early morning and there is a gentle spring rain falling. I'm glad I cut my lawn yesterday, for the rest of this week we may have rain.

I'm finding *Wounded Prophet: A Portrait of Henri J.M. Nouwen*, to be a real gem. There are two things I wish to discuss this morning.

First, in his *Bread for the Journey* (London: Darton, Longman and Todd, 1996), Nouwen writes:

> As we simply sit down in front of a sheet of paper and start to express in words what is in our minds or in our hearts, new ideas emerge, ideas that can surprise us and lead us to inner places we hardly knew were there. One of the most satisfying aspects of writing is that it can open in us deep wells of hidden treasures that are beautiful for us as well as for others to see (136).

What wonderful words those are to a writer! I find that when I begin writing my daily journal, my problem is not thinking of something to say. On the contrary! I find that so much happens in my daily life as a parish priest that I have to weed out most of my life experiences and focus on just a couple of thoughts or events that stand out in my mind. I also love Nouwen's idea that the hidden treasures that the writer puts on paper will be beautiful to others. I hope someday people find these journals helpful.

I am so impressed by Nouwen's idea that a wealth of treasures were inside him, not something that could be found in a library. After all, when one is looking to explain "reality" from the heart, the only source can be from self. Sometimes I forget my own rich bank of life experiences: university teaching all my adult life since I was 25 years old; practicing every area of nursing (except operating room) since I was 22 years old; writing and research in sociology and chemical dependency nursing; living in many parts of the United States; giving numerous research papers in Europe and South America; experiencing missions in Central America and Africa; and my spectacular and scary adventures in the depths of alcoholism and sobriety. Wow! Have I got plenty to say!

I ask the Holy Spirit today and in the future to guide me in my writing so that I may touch others' lives – especially those of parish priests.

The *National Catholic Reporter* called around 11:00 a.m. and said they are interested in doing a piece based on my "Defensive Ministry" article.

They felt that it contains much practical advice on practicing safer ministry and that priests would benefit from it.

April 11, 2002 – Thursday
Wake Forest, N.C.
68 F – Mostly sunny

What an incredibly interesting day this has been – a day full of joy and sadness and energy.

The sad thing was that the bishop removed a priest friend of mine (Fr. X) from active ministry. Apparently, the priest had sex with a minor 41 years ago and also 15 years ago. On his yearly form that we are all required to complete, my friend said he had never been arrested for sex with a minor. This was untrue. The diocesan policy required that my friend be removed from active ministry not only for sex with minors, but also for lying on a form in seminary and in priesthood. Unfortunately, this priest is a troubled person, but he has incredible love in his heart. I will pray for him every day. How incredibly devastated he must feel at this time.

On a brighter note, I received word from Duke University that I have been appointed Associate Consulting Professor in Nursing, effective May 1, 2002 through June 30, 2003. The letter is a bit confusing because it comes from a physician and welcomes me to the faculty of the Duke University School of Medicine. Somehow, the schools of nursing and medicine must be related. At The University of Iowa, they were two very separate entities. Anyway, I'm happy to have a university affiliation as I have had one almost my whole adult life since I was 25 years old.

This evening, I addressed the St. Catherine of Siena Home & School Association, which would be called the PTA in most places. An incredibly negative person in the parent population is a saboteur. I warned the community about negativity and how it drains valuable energy. I pointed out that my philosophy, which I call the "St. Catherine way," is that we ask excellent people to do excellent work in a spirit of joy with kindness towards all. I think the meeting went very well. We had lively discussion from 7:30 p.m. to 9:00 p.m.

April 12, 2002 – Friday
Wake Forest, N.C.
Cloudy – 74 F

My schedule was excellent today. After 8:45 a.m. Mass, my schedule was free. I decided to put new plants above the altar and they turned out pretty nicely.

All through the day, however, I kept thinking of Fr. X and how devastated he must be to be relieved of his priestly ministry. His case was in the newspaper this morning, and it's been on the news every hour. Though I understand the diocesan stand on sex with minors, I can't help but wonder where the mercy and compassion is with something that happened so many years ago, long before Fr. X was even a Catholic! Perhaps God has a monopoly on mercy in the case of sex with minors when it involves priests; the Church seems to have run out of mercy. How terrible to have one's life shattered by events long gone. God help my friend.

This morning, I told the Wake Forest Cultural Arts Commission that I would be interested in serving on their board. They said that they have Presbyterians and Baptists on the board but no Catholics. Since St. Catherine's is the largest congregation in Wake Forest by far, they are excited that there will be a Catholic representation. My position has to be approved by the whole board first, but I doubt there will be a problem getting on. I've never been on an arts commission before, so it should be interesting. The board meets for two hours on Monday from September through May. I hope to meet more people and to deepen my roots in this community.

April 13, 2002 – Saturday
Wake Forest, N.C.
Cloudy – low 70s F

When I went out to get the newspaper from my driveway this morning, I discovered a package in my mailbox. It turned out to be the book I ordered from Amazon.Com called, *Salvation on Sand Mountain: Snake Handling and Redemption in Southern Appalachia*, by Dennis Covington (NY:

Penguin Books, 1995). I saw a special on this group of snake handlers two weeks ago and heard about the book. I think this will be a fascinating read.

Fr. X is again in the newspaper today. The article interviews some of Fr. X's parishioners, and they tell how beloved he was to them. One person said, "He made you feel so welcome and so important to the church. He was a bubbly, outgoing person."

In the paper this morning was a wonderful gem. In Ann Landers' column, former Secretary of the Treasury Robert Rubin was standing in the company of much taller members of the Cabinet. Rubin was a very short man. When asked how he felt standing next to all these tall people, he responded, "Like a dime among the pennies." How clever!

April 13, 2002 – Saturday
Wake Forest, N.C. – 8:25 p.m.
Sunny – 72 F

What a joyful day it was today! I had three Masses, and baptisms of six children—four Hispanic and two Anglo. The weather couldn't have been nicer—sunny, warm and a gentle breeze.

In the morning, I went to Bob and Betty Horky's farm and thoroughly enjoyed myself. Many of the pillars of the St. Catherine community were present. It seems that this group has been meeting for many years and they usually go to a mountain in Western North Carolina. For some reason, this year they decided not to go the mountains. Fr. Frank Moeslein, a retired priest living in the coastal city of Morehead City, N.C. was there and concelebrated Mass with me. We had Mass under a tent.

After Mass, we had a picnic featuring chicken and pork (which I didn't eat) plus all the trimmings. The people were truly wonderful and I was honored to be asked to celebrate this special occasion with them.

When I returned to the church, the Hispanics were just leaving the building. Their retreat apparently went very well, and they were filled with the Spirit. God, I just love the Hispanic community!

The 5:00 p.m. Mass went well. The St. Catherine Latino band played and, as always, the Anglos liked them. Well, most of the people liked them. One woman was angry that we had the Latino band, but then you can't please everyone all the time. I apologized before Mass that I forgot to mention last Saturday that the Latino band would be playing this Saturday. There is one woman who would rather go to a Sunday Mass than to listen to the Hispanic Band. She says it is because she likes to sing along. I hope it is not out of prejudice.

I was happy to tell Sergio, one of the Hispanic leaders, that we may have found a 20-passenger bus for our church. The Hispanics especially want to have the bus to bring others to church on Sundays. I told Sergio this would be the "first of the fleet."

After the 5:00 p.m. Mass, I went to Camp Kanata to celebrate Mass with our Anglo Confirmation crowd. (The Hispanics have a separate preparation, but they will celebrate Confirmation on May 1st at St. Raphael's with the Anglos.) We celebrated Mass outdoors at an outdoor chapel under the pines overlooking the lake. Some of the members of "Soul Purpose," our praise and worship band, played for this event. Afterwards, we had snacks at the main cabin where the St. Catherine crowd is staying this weekend.

So it was quite an adventurous day, and I'm so delighted that I am a priest with so many special ways to serve the Lord and enter people's lives.

April 14, 2002 – 3rd Sunday of Easter
Wake Forest, N.C. – 7:45 p.m.
78 F – Sunny to cloudy

Well, I made it through the weekend in one piece. After seven Masses and eight baptisms, we had a celebration of the 25th wedding anniversary of two parishioners. The priest who witnessed their wedding 25 years ago, a Redemptorist from Puerto Rico, assisted me with the ceremony.

I told the priest about my interest in getting some Puerto Rican masks for decorating my walls, and he said his order has a house near a town where there are plenty of masks. He gave me his email address, so I just might take him up on it and fly down there sometime. I could use a small vacation.

This weekend, Bishop Gossman declared April 14, 2002 as "A Day of Prayer for the Church in Crisis." I read a letter from the bishop at all the Masses in English; Rosa read the letter in Spanish at our Mass in Spanish. I hope that the current crisis brings good things and not more evil. I'm happy to learn that American Catholics are rallying around their priests and are not driven out of the Church by the scandal. Here at St. Catherine's, we have had nine new families join this past week.

Summer-like weather has come to the Triangle area. Today it was 78 degrees. Although we were supposed to have lots of rain and thunderstorms, it was basically sunny all day except for a brief period of rain. I love the warm weather and being able to run around in shorts and T-shirts when I'm not in my clerical garb, which I wear most of the time. Tomorrow, I think I'll plant some geraniums on my deck in honor of the great weather! Later in the week, it is supposed to be in the upper 80s F. Hallelujah!

April 15, 2002 – Monday (Tax Day)
Wake Forest, N.C. – 7:30 p.m.
Partly sunny – 81 F

This morning, I was delighted to receive an email from Fr. X. He says he's in the anger mode right now but that he feels in time he will be well. He sees himself as the sacrificial lamb of the Diocese of Raleigh. I pray that somehow this horrible tragedy in his life will lead to a life filled with meaning and joy. How that can happen I don't have any idea—but with God, all things are possible.

April 16, 2002 – Tuesday
Wake Forest, NC – 9:00 p.m.
Sunny – 90 F

As I write this, I'm still a bit groggy. This morning, I had a couple of teeth removed under sedation, and this evening, I took some codeine for pain. I love having dental work when I'm asleep. When I'm awake, I'm the worst patient in the world! Thank God I found Dr. Barker.

Don (our custodian) took me to the dentist this morning, and while waiting for my appointment, I began reading *Salvation on Sand Mountain*. Though I'm only in the beginning chapters, I can tell the book is well written. I'm looking forward to continuing it.

Yesterday, the workers finally came to St. Catherine's and began to work on the lower parking lot. When it is finished, our parish will be very grateful! Gael and I talked about putting small ornamental trees separating the upper from lower parking lot. I believe that would look very nice.

Some of our staff members went on field trips to look at offices at Faith Baptist Church in Youngsville, N.C. and St. Andrew's Catholic Church in Apex, N.C.. All of our field trips must be done by May 2nd when we will take all our data and put our parish self-study together.

Last evening, I gave the invocation for the city council meeting at Wake Forest Town Hall. Before the meeting, I got to meet a new city worker in town by the name of Steven. I gave him plenty of positive strokes for being so helpful to St. Catherine's and his very prompt reply to our request. Usually, it takes forever and a day to get any response from the town! He said he arrived in town in January and is enjoying his job very much. Besides his wife, he has a 4-year-old daughter. Steven is helping Gael and myself with finding the right place to build a rectory on Tyler Run.

After the council meeting, we had Parish Council. The theme of the council last evening was our financial picture. Basically, St. Catherine's is in great shape financially, but our offertory needs to be beefed up. Part of the reason our offertory isn't growing as fast as we want is because many people who are strapped for cash are giving generously to our capital campaign.

April 19, 2002 – Thursday
Wake Forest, N.C. – 10:30 a.m.
91 F – Sunny

Yesterday, I received the latest edition of the *National Catholic Reporter* (Vol. 38, No. 24, April 19, 2002), and there was an article called "'Defensive Ministry' Necessary, Priest Says" on page four. It was a pretty well-written article on my original "Defensive Ministry" article that appeared in *The Priest* in 1997, but they said that St. Catherine's is in Raleigh instead of Wake Forest. Oh, well, nobody's perfect. Now the editor of *NC Catholics* wants to do an article on the topic, and I'll be happy to oblige.

The St. Catherine campus is a flurry of activity this morning! On the west side of the East Campus, the parking lot is under construction, while on the east side of the East Campus, the workers are busy building the Trinity Center. Plus, we're hosting a diocesan Development Directors' conference. The diocese is very pleased with the turnout. They expected that we would be lucky to have 20 people show up. Instead, we have 40 principals and development directors. I'm delighted that we are playing host to this group! St. Catherine's is one of only a handful of parishes in the Diocese of Raleigh that has a development director.

As if our construction projects and conference aren't enough, three of our Knights of Columbus are busy building six picnic tables for us. These tables are their gift to the parish, and they are planning on having them completed in time for our Parish Picnic and Ministry Fair on Sunday, April 28th – the day before the Feast of St. Catherine of Siena. Our council does so much work with so few men involved. God bless them!

Last evening, I held an anointing Mass where I administered the Sacrament of the Sick after the homily. We had 165 people, so the Mass took almost an hour. Usually, our daily Masses only take about 20 minutes. Next year, I'll invite Fr. Des to come and help out.

This morning, I finished reading Fr. Andrew Greeley's *Letters to a Loving God: A Prayer Journal.* I was interested to learn that when he is writing a novel, he averages 2,000 words per day—which works out to about eight pages of 250 words each. I hope that someday I, too, will become more prolific.

The newspaper reported today that Fr. Y, a very popular priest and one of my favorites, was removed by the bishop because of sex with a minor that occurred a quarter of a century ago! Where is mercy? Where is forgiveness? I think the dioceses is becoming so gun-shy that they are willing to destroy marvelous lives to cover themselves from lawsuits. God bless Fr. Y and keep him from further harm. May this horrible life change bring some kind of blessings to him.

April 20, 2002 – Saturday
Wake Forest, N.C. – 10:00 a.m.
90 F – Sunny with possible thunderstorms

One of the best things that happened on Thursday was a meeting with Eric H. He is a very fine young man who is very successful in life and has an excellent grasp of his faith. He believes very strongly that of those who have much, much will be expected. That's great news, as I asked him to be the one in charge of heading some capital campaigns to raise the one-third down payment we need for our new sanctuary and office building. When he said yes, I experienced a tremendous load off my back. I believe Eric will do a super job, and I am ready to help in any way I can—even if it means personally visiting hundreds of homes!

I received a note from Adam W. today. He's finishing up his first year of law school at American University in Washington, D.C., and he is going to be studying cross-cultural issues and inter-American trade this summer. I'm delighted he's doing so well, but then I knew he would. Adam hopes to one day be the second Catholic Democratic President of the United States. When he gets elected, he's going to send for me to be the "First Priest." What a great idea for a novel, no? I hope he makes it!

April 22, 2002 – Monday
Wake Forest, N.C. – 11:30 a.m.
Cloudy – 80s F

What a great weekend it was here at St. Catherine's! Fr. Dave La Buda, the co-pastor of our sister parish in San Pedro Sula, Honduras preached at all the Masses. He preached on the concept of hope and how the little projects add up to give hope to those who are very poor—people that he serves. Among Holy Trinity Parish's projects are tattoo removals for former gang members, building houses for the poor and starting a new Montessori kindergarten. Gang members need to have their tattoos removed so they can get jobs. Since the program started, over 9,000 people have had their tattoos removed. The program has been so successful, in fact, that Holy Trinity parish is opening tattoo removal clinics in Guatemala City and in El Salvador! Last fall, the program even made international news when featured on CNN. The people loved having him here.

On Saturday evening, the Fourth Degree Knights of Columbus came to the 5:00 p.m. Mass and made a presentation of a chalice to Jean Swiderski, widow of Joe Swiderski. Jean, in turn, gave the chalice to our parish. The base of the chalice is inscribed with Joe's name. Joe was a wonderful parishioner who was an usher until he could no longer walk.

After Mass, one of the little girls of the parish came up to tell me how much she liked having "the pirates" at Mass. Because the Knights were decked out in their plumes and feathers and other regalia, they looked like pirates to her.

After the 5:00 p.m. Mass, our two Maryknoll Affiliates who are going to Honduras in May took Fr. Dave and me out to dinner at Safari Grill. Dave informed the two women about conditions in San Pedro Sula and assured them that they would be very welcome. I hope that we will be able to send some of our teens down there next summer to help former gang members build houses for the poor.

In the afternoon, Fr. Dave left for Wilmington, N.C. where he is staying with his sister. Also, my dear friend David Sanchez came for a visit. David will be ordained as a priest in the Archdiocese of Louisville on June 8th, and I will preach at his First Mass of Thanksgiving on June 9th. We went out to dinner, watched a movie and talked about priesthood. This morning, David joined me in serving as the deacon for our daily Mass. I'm glad the people are getting a flavor of different ministerial types, as I'm the only ordained priest in the parish.

April 25, 2002 – Thursday
Wake Forest, N.C. – 9:00 a.m.
Breezy, sunny and partly cloudy – low 70s F

As I write this, it's morning at the office. I sit at my computer in front of a huge window overlooking the hills and woods of our campus. The trees are all green now, and there are many irises and azaleas in full bloom. It's all very nice.

I was up at 5:00 a.m. this morning and could not go back to sleep. I think that all the craziness of the world right now, plus the stresses of running a fast-growing parish, might be the cause of waking up so early. I have not been able to write in this journal for the past few days because my life has been so hectic—wonderful, but hectic, nevertheless.

Last evening, I went to a house near St. Raphael's parish in Raleigh to anoint an elderly woman who had just arrived from New York. She was staying with her daughter and is going to have a cardiac catheterization today.

On my way home, I learned that a priest in a neighboring parish where I have celebrated Advent and Lenten Reconciliation Services has been put on administrative leave by the bishop for past sexual abuse allegations. Fr. Z is a good man and I pray that he will be okay.

The big news of the day is that the United States cardinals have been meeting with the pope about the sex abuse scandal. There are so many people clamoring with their concerns and "solutions" to the problem that it is very depressing. Everybody thinks they are experts, it seems!

John Strange, editor of *NC Catholics*, interviewed me on Tuesday morning about my ideas about "Defensive Ministry." He is going to do a piece in the next issue of *NC Catholics*. He didn't read my article on "Defensive Ministry" before his interview because he wanted to have an open mind and fresh approach. I encouraged him, however, to read the article before he writes his own article. After all, not everything can be covered in a newspaper article.

On Monday, I had lunch with Wayne Davies at the Hong Kong Restaurant in Wake Forest. Wayne's job is to look after the welfare of the priests of the Diocese of Raleigh. This service is provided to every priest, free of charge; the Diocese of Raleigh pays for this service. He does evaluations of various life realms: law, health, living conditions, finances, retirement planning and the like. He is anxious to help in any way. For example, he told of how a particular priest wanted a particular car with a certain color and, of course, he wanted to get the best deal on the car. Wayne arranged it so that the new car was delivered to the priest's driveway, and the car dealer took the priest's old car away as a trade-in. Now that's what I call service!

On Tuesday, the chancellor of the diocese, the diocesan attorney, and the construction and property manager all came to St. Catherine's because we have been building our Trinity Center without any contracts signed by the bishop. Well, it turned out that, indeed, we did have contracts, but the man who signed them for us simply did not know to send them on to the bishop. I assured the men that here at St. Catherine's, I am a new pastor and our business manager is new. We want to follow all the rules, and anytime we don't, it is only because we didn't know to do something. I reminded them that we look to them for help and need their help. A parish that has not built many buildings, we have not learned the process as bigger parishes have. They were very fine with that and all went well. I was elated that the day turned out so well since I had worried all day about the meeting.

April 27, 2002 – Saturday
Wake Forest, N.C. – 7:00 a.m.
Partly cloudy – chance of rain – 70 F

This morning, I awoke around 3:30 a.m. and could not get back to sleep. Like the last few nights, I have been having very intense dreams. Last night, I dreamt that I was saying goodbye to people in Missoula, Montana (where I did my Ph.D. studies), and then saying goodbye to fellow staff members at Harborview Medical Center in Seattle where I practiced psychiatric nursing while doing my doctoral research.

I think the inability to sleep is related to the loss of three fine priests in our diocese. Perhaps that is why I have dreamt of saying goodbye. Who knows? But part of my insomnia, I think, is related to the increasingly hostile environment created by anti-gay bigots who are writing in the newspaper. They are equating pedophilia in the Catholic priesthood with gay men. They go on to justify the anti-gay bigotry espoused by the Boy Scouts of America. Many of these pro-hate writers are furious that the Triangle United Way has removed the Boy Scouts from the annual appeal process because of the scouts' anti-gay bigotry stance. Good for the United Way! Bigotry makes me sick!

Yesterday, I talked with Fr. Matt at St. Mark's in Wilmington. We set up May 11th and 12th as a mission weekend when I would preach at all the Masses at St. Mark's. I'll tell the people about the missionary efforts St. Catherine's is doing and ask for their financial help. It will be terrific to see the wonderful people of St. Mark's once again. It is true that a priest's first assignment is very special to him. I could not have asked for a better place to have had my first two years of priesthood.

On a bright note, I received a note from dear parishioners with a newspaper clipping attached – sort of a homemade greeting card. The newspaper clipping was signed simply, "A practicing Catholic." The clip reads as follows:

> The current crisis of our church tests our faith and questions the integrity of the priesthood. A few men who have forgotten their vows have cast a pall over all priests. The vast majority continues to do your job every day in spite of the criticism you get from the media and some parishioners. In times like this, we need to remember and be grateful for the great sacrifices you make every day to bring our church to those in need.
>
> - Thank you for your anointed hands that hold the body and blood of Jesus Christ every day
> - Thank you for the hours you spend preparing homilies, spiritual exercises and presentations to help us better understand the word of God
> - Thank you for the wisdom of counsel, guidance and forgiveness you bring us through the sacrament of penance
> - Thank you for the hours of sleep and relaxation you have given up to be present when a dying person needs the last rites and your comfort
> - Thank you for the hours of prayer, counsel and encouragement you give to friends and family in times of pain, sorrow and joy
> - Thank you for the many hours you spend encouraging, guiding and facilitating the many ministries that enrich the spiritual, temporal and social life of our community
> - Thank you for the many times you did not eat or ate alone because someone needed you at mealtime
> - Thank you for the vow of celibacy you accepted to provide time to dedicate your life to be a shepherd of our flock. May the Lord bless and keep you.

A practicing Catholic

What a wonderful message. May I always live up to what an ideal priest should be!

I continue to read *The Wounded Prophet* and find the life of Fr. Henri Nouwen very fascinating. Like Fr. Andrew M. Greeley and Fr. Thomas Merton, I am amazed at how much life Nouwen was able to pack into a lifetime! When I read about these prolific writers and mystics, I feel so very small and wasteful with my time and talents. I pray that my renewed writing in this journal will spill over into my other writing projects and get me on the road to using my talents wisely. Watching TV for hours on end needs to stop—although I do get many ideas from some of the shows and find this relaxing.

April 29, 2002 – Monday – Feast of St. Catherine of Siena
Wake Forest, N.C. – 9:00 p.m.
Sunny – 70s F

Well, we had a beautiful day for our picnic after all. The sun came out in full force, and a great breeze came through keeping the temperatures bearable. We had at least 500 people, including many Hispanic brothers and sisters. I think the Anglos and Hispanics enjoyed each other's presence, and I believe both peoples find St. Catherine's to be their parish home. I am so blessed to be the priest of such a place!

The school kids came to Mass today to celebrate our parish's patron saint. I gave a special blessing to the school's volunteers, and the principal gave each a lapel pin to wear. Afterwards, we had a small reception of breakfast food.

The bishop called a special meeting of all the priests of the diocese for May 8th. Naturally, that's my day off! Anyway, we're all supposed to meet at the Short Journey Center in Smithfield, N.C. The topic, I'm sure, is the sex abuse scandal—real and imagined—plaguing our country and diocese. I hope it is a healing meeting and not something that simply makes a bad situation worse.

Today, I began working at a furious pace on our parish self-study. Getting it all done in time will be a miracle! I think I'll have to spend several hours a day all this week to make it all happen. I hope the Diocese of Raleigh Building & Real Estate Commission likes it. I'm anxious to get our architects here to begin designing our campuses. Then we can begin to do some mini-campaigns for raising the one-third down payment that we need.

April 30, 2002 – Tuesday
Wake Forest, N.C. – 6:00 p.m.
Sunny – 70s F

This past weekend, I noticed one of our Hispanic community leaders, Sergio, listening to a young woman practicing reading in Spanish from the ambo. She sounded great to me. Therefore, I was very surprised to hear her practicing from the ambo the very next day. I learned later, however, that she has been chosen to read the epistle in Spanish tomorrow night at St. Raphael's for our Confirmation ceremony.

I reflect this evening on what that honor must mean to her, and what will go through her mind and heart tomorrow evening as she sees the hundreds of people from different areas of our deanery begin arriving at St. Raphael's. What will go through her mind when she hears the thunderous music and witnesses the huge procession of *Confirmandi*, servers, priests and bishop? I imagine she will be very nervous indeed!

As a priest, I'm in the spotlight each day. On the weekends, I preach to about 1,500 people here at St. Catherine's. As I near my fourth anniversary of ordination to priesthood, I don't get very nervous anymore. Thus, sometimes I forget what an awesome thing it is for laypersons to participate in special ways in the liturgy. Even bringing up the gifts of bread and wine may be the highlight of a person's week! When I reflect on this, I am so very humbled. The infinite supply of riches I enjoy as a priest I often take for granted. I forget how precious those riches are to those who only get small morsels of them now and again in liturgical celebrations. May I never forget what a joy it is for others to have a special role in liturgy.

Today, I spent most of the day preparing for our self-study. I was able to finish the mission-sister parish section and, yesterday, I got the liturgy section done. Though we are spending a lot of time on this project, I believe we will look back on it with great joy when it's finished. I just hope the Diocese of Raleigh Building & Real Estate Commission likes it!

MAY 2002

May 1, 2002 – Wednesday – St. Joseph the Worker
Wake Forest, N.C. – 9:45 p.m.
Sunny – 70s F

Earlier in the day, I was mostly in a gloomy state—nothing serious, but gloomy just the same. The day brightened up considerably, however, when I left to go to the Confirmation dinner with the bishop and other priests. Before I got there, however, I stopped off at In His Name Catholic store and picked up a couple of crucifixes for our two missionaries.

This evening, however, was wonderful. We had Confirmation at St. Raphael's, and everyone was amazed at how many of those being confirmed were from St. Catherine's. We had almost as many as St. Raphael's had, and they are more than triple the size of our parish. The ceremony was very beautiful.

I arrived at St. Raphael's early, but that was good. I was able to visit with my spiritual director who is Pastor of that parish. We shared our concerns about the sex scandals.

May 2, 2002 – Thursday
Wake Forest, N.C. – 10:00 a.m.
Partly Cloudy – 70s F

Today, I received a Spiritual Bouquet from a man in Carthage, N.C. It's a form letter, but it was personalized for me. It appears that many lay people around the diocese are making a Novena to St. John Vianney, (Patron Saint of Parish Priests) for the priests of the Diocese of Raleigh. What a great thing!

Our St. Catherine of Siena Catalogue of Gifts has finally been printed and it looks terrific. It lists the various ministries at St. Catherine's with a brief description of each. Each ministry has a logo to make it more pleasing to the eye. For example, our "Sister Parishes' Ministry" features the flags of Honduras and Uganda – the countries where our two sister parishes are located.

May 4, 2002 – Saturday
Wake Forest, N.C. – 8:20 a.m.
Rainy and cool – highs in the low to mid 50s F

A cold snap has come through the area, so today it is not supposed to get above the mid-50s. Then we'll be back into the 70s and 80s F by tomorrow. Strange weather!

Two great quotes of the day come from Ann Landers' column: "Resentment is letting someone you despise live rent-free in your head." How true! Another person wrote in about how to deal with religious bigots who claim the "unbeliever" will be going to hell. The person should respond with, "Thank you. I'm so glad we'll be neighbors." If only we had more wisdom and humor in the world instead of hatred and anger.

I had a nice talk with the vicar general yesterday. He hopes that our meeting with the bishop this coming Wednesday will encourage healing among the priests. There is much sadness among the priests over the three priests who were relieved of their active ministries.

Yesterday, I glanced at a special article in *Newsweek* (May 6, 2002). The cover of this edition is "What Would Jesus Do? Beyond the Priest Scandal: Christianity at the Crossroads." The section on celibacy and marriage has some very intriguing statistics – statistics that back up Fr. Andrew M. Greeley's findings that Catholics tend to be much more progressive than their Protestant counterparts on many issues. For example, this article shows that in a *Newsweek* poll, Catholics "narrowly oppose legally sanctioning gay marriages, 47 percent to 44 percent, but they are more liberal than non-Catholics, 61 percent of whom don't think such marriages are a good idea." The article goes on to say, "Meanwhile, Catholics in the United States are more likely than non-Catholics to accept a homosexual priest in a committed relationship with someone of the same sex, 39 percent to 29 percent" (29).

The vicar general encouraged me to speak out at the bishop's meeting with the priests. As he said, it would be a shame if the meeting were only one way. He hopes, as do I, that priests will express their thoughts and feelings.

May 5, 2002 – 6th Sunday of Easter
Wake Forest, N.C. – 5:30 a.m.
Cloudy to partly sunny – to be around 72 F

This quote was in my email this morning and is about good preaching. I couldn't agree more!

> "Indeed, any sermon that remained entirely in the realm of abstract thought, never touching the real world of field and crops, parents and children, employers and workers, feasts and banquets, toil and play, would hardly qualify as Christian preaching at all."
> - Thomas Long in *The Witness of Preaching*

May 6, 2002 – Monday
Wake Forest, N.C. – 8:00 p.m.
Partly cloudy – 70 F

It was another busy weekend, but a good one. Three of the five Masses were First Holy Communion Masses, so we had the usual flurry of photos—each child and myself, group shots, shots with parents and grandparents, and the like. Naturally, after every First Holy Communion Mass we also had a reception. I only got to one of the receptions because I was busy greeting people.

We also had a wedding, four baptisms and blessing ceremonies for our first two Maryknoll Affiliates whom we are sending to a foreign land. Missionaries Sandy Litz and Arlene Fisher will be leaving for San Pedro Sula, Honduras tomorrow. I'm very excited about this, as I have been waiting for this day for a long time.

I'm still working fast and furious trying to get the self-study together. By the end of the week, I should be worn out—just in time to travel to Wilmington, N.C. to preach all weekend at St. Mark's!

May 7, 2002 – Tuesday
Wake Forest, N.C. – 7:15 a.m.
Partly cloudy – high to be around 82 F

As I begin this day, I am very happy with the news delivered to me via this email:

> For the second year in a row, the *NC Catholic* and the Diocese of Raleigh's *Propagation of the Faith*, directed by Father William Pitts, have won first place in the Archbishop Edward T. O'Meara Awards. We won for the eight-page, *"The Field Afar,"* published October 21, an intriguing account of Father Bob Kus' mission visit to Uganda.
>
> The special supplement features Father Bob's well-written stories of the people and churches of Uganda, along with his photos, Tammy Stanley's graphic design that tied it all together under one theme in eight pages, and judicious, measured editing by yours truly.
>
> The award will be presented at the Catholic Press Association conference later this month in Minneapolis.
>
> Congratulations to all involved!

When I get the self-study done, I will have to take time to send the five articles included in *The Field Afar* to *Catholic Digest*. Hopefully, they will find at least one of the articles worthy of printing in their magazine. They printed my article, "My Dinner with Batman" a couple of years ago when I was a seminarian.

May 8, 2002 – Wednesday
Wake Forest, N.C. – 6:15 p.m.
Mostly sunny – 85 F

Today, all the priests of our diocese went to the Short Journey Retreat Center in Smithfield, N.C. to spend time with the bishop. After a prayer service, the bishop talked about how hard the last three weeks have been on him due to putting three priests on administrative leave. He said this is the saddest time he's ever experienced in the 27 years he has been Bishop of Raleigh.

After the bishop spoke, the priests had their say. I was quite amazed at how deeply the men have been thinking and the amazing facility so many of them had in expressing themselves. The priests seemed to be angry at the process we have in place. They also believe that things that happened many years ago should be ancient history. My contribution to the discussion was to encourage the bishop to add an alcoholism expert to his Bishop's Advisory Council. I pointed out that many men who are alcoholic do things in their drinking days that they would never dream of doing when living in sobriety. I said that I believe that many of the sexual indiscretions that may have been done in the distant past with some priests may have been done while the men were actively drinking, but now they have been sober many years. An expert on the panel would ensure that the Advisory Council would be able to distinguish between an alcoholic indiscretion and a serial pedophile. The bishop agreed, and others thanked me for my contribution.

I was most impressed by Fr. Mike from the coast who told of how a statute of limitations has a firm and wise foundation in law. He pointed out, in effect, that if a person must go through his entire life with the baggage of the past, he couldn't truly live a life.

The surprise of the day was that Fr. X came to the meeting. He got up early in the meeting and told the bishop that he loved him and forgave him, and that "Zero tolerance is zero Christ." He then sat down. Fr. X said all this with tremendous anger in his tone.

Last evening, our development director made a wonderful presentation at our Parish Council on fundraising. She gave us many new ideas – ideas that we'll discuss further when this self-study is finally mailed!

As if the stress of getting the self-study is not enough, I have had two other hot-button issues dumped in my lap.

The first is the issue of gender equality in the school. I support gender equality 100 percent, but others do not. The physical education teacher and principal want to ban members of one sex from participating in various groups. For example, I said I wouldn't give my okay for a female-only cheerleader club. I pointed out that if only girls wanted to join, that would be okay. But if just one boy wanted to join, the group would have to allow him to join. Likewise, in the future, if a girl wants to join a boys' sports team, she must be allowed to join. If the diocesan conference throws out a St. Catherine team because we practice gender equality, so be it. Now, the principal is going to bring the P.E. teacher to try to talk me into sex discrimination.

The second issue is a group of families in our parish who are homeschoolers. They want the parish to recognize them as a regular group of St. Catherine's. We cannot do that because to do so, we are saying that we agree with what they are teaching about our religion. In fact, we do not know what they are teaching. Furthermore, there is evidence that many of them are using outdated materials that our diocese does not recommend. By removing themselves and their children from the control of St. Catherine's Pastor and Faith Formation Program, they can hardly be seen as a St. Catherine group.

May 15, 2002 – Wednesday – St. Isidore the Farmer
Wake Forest, N.C. – 5:30 p.m.
Sunny – 74 F

As I write this, I have just celebrated my usual Wednesday home Mass, and all is peaceful here.

The last six days have been the most difficult and scary of my priesthood to date.

Last Friday, I received a call from a former employee of St. Catherine's who is given to rage reactions. She called to let me know that she had seen my name on the Internet in conjunction with gay-related things. It turns out that she saw some of my writings advertised. She was her usual self: intense hatred wrapped up in a fury of rage—pure evil. She wouldn't listen to my explanation that my specialties in sociology and nursing are gay men's studies and alcohol studies, and that I wrote those things while a professor. In her twisted mind, anything having to do with gay people must be evil. Thus, in her mind, I am evil. I finally hung up on her when I realized I was dealing with pure evil.

I called up the vicar general immediately, and he told me she had contacted him. He told her that the diocese knew all about my writings and my academic career and that there was no problem.

I don't know if that will calm her down enough or not. Since Friday, I have been wondering what would happen if she would write a letter to the editor of the Catholic or Raleigh newspaper. I'm sure life would be most interesting. I have done nothing wrong, but at the same time, there are people filled with homophobia and other forms of evil just waiting to cause harm to innocent people.

I only pray that I may always be a priest in good standing with the Church all the days of my life.

With that heavy burden from Friday, I spent the weekend in Wilmington, N.C. where I preached at all the Masses at St. Mark's, my first priesthood parish. I preached about the missions, focusing especially on my experiences in Uganda. The people took up a second collection for the mission work we are doing at St. Catherine's. It was good seeing everyone again, but my heart was very heavy after the vicious phone call. Fr. Matt was wonderful to talk with, and he helped soothe my spirit. I slept in the apartment over the garage in the rectory, the apartment that I decorated while serving at St. Mark's.

On Monday, my secretary, Connie, and I put together our parish's self-study – all 194 pages of it! By binding it by hand, we saved a lot of money, but it took us five hours and 45 minutes to complete it! It looks magnificent.

Today, I firmed up the mission trip schedule for Jeff Garrett and Anne Perrotta, our Maryknoll Affiliates. They'll go to Uganda in October and come back in November.

May 17, 2002 – Friday
Wake Forest, N.C. – 7:10 a.m.
Sunny – 84 F

The other day, I finished reading Michael Ford's *Wounded Prophet: A Portrait of Henri J.M. Nouwen*. What an excellent book it was! I hated to see it end. I am now going to read more of Nouwen's works. I just ordered *¡Gracias! A Latin American Journal* from Amazon.com. I love to read about interesting people who struggle with life and come out victorious. Henri struggled with accepting his gay sexual orientation, and this struggle made him more sensitive towards others. Eventually, he was able to accept his gay self as a divine gift – something to be treasured and celebrated instead of something to be ashamed.

Yesterday morning, I met with a former mayor of Wake Forest. He is the realtor who is trying to buy the westernmost five acres of land from St. Catherine's. The plan for the builder is to build a community of 40 townhouses ranging from the $140,000 to $170,000 price range. It will be called Siena Park. I know that our parish would love to keep the land, but on the other hand, I know that it would be the more ethical thing to sell the land even if the city of Wake Forest does not get all the approvals needed by June 30th – the date our contract is set to expire. Perhaps we can get a bit more money if we renegotiate after June 30th. Even if we sell the five acres out of the 20.5 acres we bought and are calling our West Campus, we still have about 14 new acres. That, combined with our 20 plus acres, should give us all the land we need to build our dream campus.

Yesterday, the priests of the Raleigh Deanery met at Our Lady of Lourdes and had a great session talking about the priest sex scandals and how they are affecting us personally. I am happy to note that most of the priests seem to be very much in favor of changing the way accused priests are treated. We agree that they have been treated very poorly. We also learned that the pastor of a Cape Fear Deanery parish resigned as requested by the bishop and is going to alcoholism treatment. We prayed for the four priests who have been removed in the last two months. I was happy to learn that the diocese will continue to support the men financially.

May 21, 2002 – Tuesday
New Bern, N.C. – 3:10 p.m.
Partly cloudy – 66 F

I'm writing this from the Sheraton Grand Hotel in New Bern, N.C. where I am attending a priest conference on financial issues. I'm here for the rest and relaxation and to learn more about retirement issues.

I'm coming down with a cold but, fortunately, I had some leftover antibiotics that I'm taking. I know, I know, I shouldn't take leftover meds, but it's better than a sore throat. My room overlooks the swimming pool and also the river and marina. It is very beautiful.

The past few days have been hectic as usual, but a little more peaceful for me than a week ago. I haven't heard any more from the troublesome person who was giving me a hard time about my writings. Thanks be to God!

The other day, I received a very interesting letter from a stranger who describes himself as a "…disturbed person who hears voices." He rambles on about many topics including the fact that he's allergic to spirit people. In talking about spirit people, he says:

> I became acquainted with the "half-men" term, recently. It pertains to the spirit people who have re-entered someone elses [sic] body, in order to get out of the house, for one reason. They may not have all of their bodys [sic]. I pull them out of me, in the morning before taking a shower, with clasped hands. Especially at the elbow, and around the head. I pull them forward, although backwards would be better for them.
>
> You have them, and I have them.
>
> The Angels have knowledge, the Pope has faith. If you would hire those with a little knowledge, the Angels could deliver, in time. Perhaps 2 years. The clairvoyants you hire would have to be like me for possibly $6,000 a year or less, to tell you what they see or hear on Sunday.

The poor man goes on to tell how to deal with these spirit people:

Where can you live to get away from them [the spirit people]? I would guess that the high country of Colorado with the bright sunshine might be such a place.

I really don't know. There are a lot of people who have seen a ghost and never reported the experience to the authoritys [sic]. In this case, yourselves.

For your house, try to leave the thermostat at 64 to 66 at night. Not at 59. Leave the toilet lid up. Leave some filtered water in a dish, to drink.

They still like to eat off of food. Don't ask me what they do. You should turn out some lights at 8 PM, as they like to retire early. Don't walk in certain places after 8 PM. Your life will become better.

I always enjoy such letters from time to time.

Yesterday, Bob Neal and I went out in the woods and flagged the place where I hope he will build my rectory. It's a beautiful spot on Tyler Run, and the way we're planning it, it will be snuggled away in the woods— nice and private.

I had a great meeting last evening with our two Maryknoll Affiliates who just returned from San Pedro Sula, Honduras, and they're on fire with the Spirit! I'm glad they're going to talk with the whole Maryknoll Affiliate group on Thursday evening and the whole parish a week from this coming weekend.

This morning, before leaving Wake Forest to come to New Bern, I had two important meetings involving finances. One was to increase our offertory, and the other was to solve a budget shortfall for the school. The latter was rather easy to solve. The offertory enhancement program will be a little trickier. I invited Erik Hector to be part of our offertory enhancement group as he needs to learn more about our parish's finances because he will head up our capital campaigns in the fall.

May 28, 2002 – Tuesday
Wake Forest, N.C. – 8:15 a.m.
Sunny – 84 F

As I write this, I sit in my office looking out on the rolling hills of our East Campus. I think I'm finally getting over my cough. I had to leave the finance conference on Wednesday morning because I coughed steadily for 45 minutes.

Today, I present the parish's self-study and plans for the rectory to the Diocese of Raleigh Building & Real Estate Commission . I hope all goes well. The chairs of the finance and pastoral councils are joining me, as is our business manager. If all goes well, we will then be able to contact the architects to design the campus.

The only fly in the ointment, so to speak, is the uncertainty regarding the five acres of land that we are supposed to sell to a builder. According to our contract, the deal is off after June 30th. I learned a few days ago that the Town of Wake Forest would not be able to finish its work by June 30th. I think deep down in my heart I would like to keep the land for our parish. I pray that I make the right decision. I'll be asking for advice from the different councils and staff.

I'm enjoying reading Henri Nouwen's *¡Gracias! A Latin American Journal*. In many ways, the feelings and thought patterns Henri describes about himself reflect my own thought patterns and feelings.

Sunday, I went to the baccalaureate program that the Wake Forest Ministerial Association held for the Wake Forest-Rolesville High School graduates at the Wake Forest Baptist Church. It was a pretty good service, but not as dynamic as the service I attended for the Wakefield High School graduates the week before.

A lot continues to happen here at St. Catherine's. On Thursday evening, Maryknoll Affiliates Sandy Litz and Arlene Fisher talked to our Maryknoll Affiliate Chapter about their adventures at our Central American sister parish, Most Holy Trinity, in San Pedro Sula, Honduras. They had a terrific time and are filled with the Spirit! Sandy wants to go to the Mexico-USA Border Experience this summer, and

Affiliate Bill is eager to go to Maryknoll, NY this summer for a special conference. Sandy and Arlene will speak at all the Masses this coming weekend.

As discussed previously, the St. Catherine's parents who are choosing to homeschool their children want to be an official organization of St. Catherine's with all the benefits of a recognized group, yet they want to follow their own religion curriculum. I told a representative of this group that if the group adopts the same religious curriculum that we use here at St. Catherine's, a curriculum recommended by the Diocese of Raleigh, and if they agree to be directly supervised by the faith development director and myself at least four times per year, I would consider recognizing them. Many of the parents who homeschool, I think, will not go along with that. Many homeschool parents believe they have knowledge superior to the rest of Catholicism. Furthermore, some of them see the Church primarily as a system of rules and regulations and hierarchies and "truth." Persons like me tend to focus more on the Church as a community of faith trying to build up the Kingdom of God on earth, a kingdom based on the triple love command of Jesus Christ. Time will tell how this all works out.

May 29, 2002 – Wednesday
Wake Forest, N.C. – 7:45 a.m.
Sunny to cloudy – 84 F

Yesterday's trip to the diocesan Building & Real Estate Commission went absolutely great! The commission members approved our parish's self-study plus the rectory plans. They also gave us positive strokes for the fine job we did on the self-study, especially the "History of St. Catherine of Siena Parish" section. Interestingly, they indicated that they were acutely aware of the population explosion of Wake Forest, and they wondered if a 1,200-seat sanctuary would be big enough. They know that St. Michael's in Cary, N.C. was too small right from the start, and they do not want to make the same mistake again. They told the St. Catherine delegation (Gael Gormaly, our Business Manager, Tom O'Larnic, our Finance Council Chair, and Wray Harrison, our Parish

Council Chair and me) that they would have to re-examine their policies about sanctuary size and get back to us. They also indicated that they were open to balconies in sanctuaries. Gael, Tom and I celebrated by going to Rock-Ola Café for lunch.

Wray, Tom and Gael all agree that in terms of the land deal, our preference is to not sell the five acres of land. If we are forced to by attorneys for the diocese, we would want a better deal than the one on the table. I will be calling the Diocese of Raleigh attorney today to let him know of our desires.

May 30, 2002 – Thursday
Wake Forest, N.C. – 4:15 p.m.
Sunny to partly cloudy – 84 F

Yesterday evening, Chris Mihans, who helps me with my computer needs, installed Windows XP Professional and America Online Version 7.0. I'm hoping this will end the errors that have plagued this computer from the time I got it. It's great to be up to the minute in the computer world!

I talked with a young priest friend today who has been assigned to the Maryknoll language school in Cochabamba, Bolivia for a year. He has ambivalent feelings about it and hopes that he is not being banished. I told him that I envy him and that that language school is one of the best in all of South America. I'd love to go there some day, perhaps on a sabbatical. I told him of the book I'm reading by Henri Nouwen called ¡Gracias! A Latin American Journal. I'm in the beginning of the book now when Nouwen is at the Maryknoll School in Cochabamba.

Just two years ago, before assigned to St. Catherine's, I asked the Priests Personnel Board to consider me for going to a Spanish-speaking country for two years. I had in the back of my mind to write a journal of my experiences much like Nouwen's book. I think that is one of the reasons why I'm enjoying the book so very much, for I'm sort of experiencing the journey through someone else's life.

Nouwen has such profound things to say. Here is one of my favorite from the book:

Ministry is entering with our human brokenness into communion with others and speaking a word of hope. This hope is not based on any power to solve the problems of those with whom we live, but on the love of God, which becomes visible when we let go of our fears of being out of control and enter into his presence in a shared confession of weakness (1983, 1993, p. 18).

May 31, 2002 – Friday – Visitation of Mary to Elizabeth
Wake Forest, N.C. – 3:30 p.m.
Sunny – 84 F

School ended today for the kids of St. Catherine's, and the teachers and students are all thrilled. The building should be much quieter for a while.

This past month has been very productive and busy. The primary accomplishment was getting our self-study completed and the rectory plans approved. On the other hand, it was a terrible month in terms of the woman who attacked me because of my academic writing. All in all, I'm thankful for the blessings I have received, yet I'm delighted this month is finally coming to a close.

This weekend, I agreed to witness a wedding at the Youngsville Baptist Church between a St. Catherine woman and her Baptist boyfriend. The young man's grandfather is a retired Baptist minister. He and I will all witness the wedding and give blessings. This evening, we'll have the rehearsal followed by a dinner at the Hilton in Raleigh. Fr. Arturo is spending the night so he will be ready to go to our ordination tomorrow morning.

In addition to the ordination of four Colombians and a man from Columbia, S.C., I have two weddings, two Confirmations, seven Baptisms (five Anglos and two Hispanics), and 20 Hispanic First Communions. Fortunately, I only have four Masses this weekend and can, therefore, attend the Baptist-Catholic wedding since Fr. Emmanuel Katongole is taking my Saturday evening Mass.

JUNE 2002

June 3, 2002 – Monday – Ugandan Martyrs
Wake Forest, N.C. – 6:30 p.m.
Sunny – 87 F

The weekend was wonderful. Though it was very busy with baptisms, weddings, and First Holy Communions, it went very well. Because Sandy and Arlene talked about their experiences as Maryknoll Affiliates in San Pedro Sula, Honduras, I didn't have to give a homily. Thus, I just had to celebrate the Masses.

On Saturday evening, I was one of three ministers at the Youngsville Baptist Church for a wedding of one of my Catholic parishioners and her Baptist boyfriend. I made friends with the pastor of the church. He told me that his congregation is part of the Cooperative Baptist Fellowship (CBF) that is much more progressive than the Southern Baptists. I invited him to come to our ecumenical service that we are having on July 16th at St. Catherine's.

Following the wedding, we had a beautiful dinner at the Wake County Shrine Club. I met Amy and Jim Walsh, two of my parishioners, there. They made my day by expressing their great love for our school and their desire to do what they can to help in fundraising activities.

Today, I was inundated with many things taking my time and energy. Though there was nothing terrible in the day, I felt my energy drained and a little sad. I reflect that in the past, each May and November, which are polar opposite months, I have experienced two weeks of a mild depression. These past two years, I have not noticed this so much, but I am always on the lookout for the appearance of the "black dragon," the name I call my depression.

I invited two of our secretaries (Connie and Susanne) to attend a special spirituality conference in February 2003 at my alma mater, St. Meinrad School of Theology. They are very excited about going there. It will be wonderful to have a couple of staff members who can experience the magic of St. Meinrad Archabbey.

June 5, 2002 – Wednesday
Wake Forest, N.C. – 5:00 p.m.
98 F – Sunny

What an incredible evening it was yesterday at the Wake Forest Town Hall! I had to be there to give official support of selling five acres of parish land. I explained to the planning board that last year, St. Catherine's decided it needed to buy 20.5 acres of land next to our property. The builder who built the houses across W. Holding Ave. had the right of first refusal on the 20.5 acres. The only way we could purchase the land was to make a deal with the builder: We would buy the land and then sell him five of the acres so he could build a 40-unit townhome complex called Siena Park.

Over 50 of the neighbors in the neighborhood showed up to protest the selling of the land. Fortunately, many of them were my parishioners, and they came to realize that in my heart of hearts I did not want to sell the land, and I was indeed on their side. To make a long story short, the planning board nixed the project. According to the Diocese of Raleigh attorney, the builder could still demand to buy the five acres, but the chance of his doing so is "99.9 percent" unlikely. After all, why would he spend a quarter of a million dollars to buy land on which he could not build his complex? The attorney said I should just be quiet about the whole thing until June 30th comes and goes, as that is the date that our contract ends. After June 30th, St. Catherine's has no obligation to sell the land.

I was thrilled to learn what great love the neighbors have for St. Catherine's! We had a wonderful time talking and I got to meet many fine folks. I am delighted about the whole thing.

On top of that, the Carolina Hurricanes hockey team won the first game in the Stanley Cup Finals. Though I don't have a single sports gene in my body, I couldn't help but be happy for the team as everyone else was rooting for the "home team" who are the underdogs in the contest between Raleigh and Detroit.

June 7, 2002 – Friday – Sacred Heart of Jesus
Wake Forest, N.C. – 7:45 a.m.
Sunny and partly cloudy – 81 F

The grass is brown and plants are having a hard time surviving. We finally had some rain last evening and during the night. Thanks be to God for the rain!

My bag is packed, and I'm just getting ready to go to church to celebrate Mass for the Feast of the Sacred Heart. From my earliest memories, I have had a devotion to the Sacred Heart. In fact, that is one of the symbols on my ordination chalice. My plane leaves for Louisville, Kentucky at 11:55 a.m. I'm delighted to attend David Sanchez's ordination tomorrow and preach at his First Mass of Thanksgiving on Sunday. Msgr. Mike Shugrue, vicar for priests, is taking my place this weekend. I'm eager to hear how he fares doing five Masses on the weekend!

June 8, 2002 – Saturday – Immaculate Heart of Mary
Louisville, Ky. – 7:00 a.m.
Hot and sunny

I am in Louisville, Ky. for David's ordination. I was on the same flight from Raleigh with Fr. Tom Watkins of Wendell, N.C. He is on sick leave until retirement and when he reaches age 65, he will be able to retire with a pension. Our mutual friends, Bob and Pat Kochie, picked us up at the airport in Louisville, as they came a day earlier by car. We're all staying at the Motel 6 on Kemmons Dr.

Last evening, we went to St. Rita's on Preston Highway where David served as a seminarian. He considers this parish his "home base." There was a large sign in front of the campus saying "Congratulations Father David Sanchez", and the other side saying "Felicidad Padre David Sanchez." David and I grilled chicken outdoors for the group while greeting people going into a nearby St. Rita building for an Al-Anon group.

Fr. Bill Martin, the pastor, is a most gracious host. Joining us were some Mexican Sisters who cook at Mundelein, where David studied for two years; David's parents and his sister and her boyfriend (all from Puerto Rico); a Hispanic couple whom I met when I was here for David's diaconate ordination last year; and a delightful man named Jim, who works for a U.S. congressman in Washington, D.C. I very much enjoyed spending time with Jim, who at one time was thinking of becoming a priest.

I finished *¡Gracias!* on the plane and have begun Frank P. Thomas' *How to Write the Story of Your Life.* I'm hoping to do more writing and it wouldn't hurt to begin writing my autobiography.

June 9, 2002 – Sunday – 10th Sunday in Ordinary Time
Louisville, Ky. – 7:00 a.m.
Sunny – Highs in the upper 80s today

The ordination was magnificent yesterday! I got a front row seat on the side with a perfect view of the altar. Because of that, I was able to take great photos of the three men ordained as they knelt in front of Archbishop Kelly. I got to sit next to Fr. Jerry Bell, who will be the pastor of David's first parish, St. Augustine's in Lebanon, Ky. Jerry and David are both going to the parish for the first time this month. The parish will have a total change of priests.

Ordained were David Sanchez, Peter Quan Do and Brian Aloysius Kenney. David is the first Hispanic and Peter is the first Vietnamese to be ordained for the Archdiocese of Louisville. Brian, whom I know from St. Meinrad School of Theology, represents the old Irish-American culture of the city.

At the Cathedral of the Assumption, I also got to see old friends and acquaintances such as Fr. Mark O'Keefe, President-Rector of St. Meinrad School of Theology, several Sisters from St. Meinrad's, and Fr. Gary Pageant, who used to do my income taxes for free at the seminary where we were both seminarians. I was especially happy to see Fr. Bill Bowling, who was a year ahead of me at St. Meinrad's. He always contributed to our School of Theology publication, *Suggested Readings*, of which I was the editor. Bill is an excellent writer and a delightful person.

After the ordination, David's family and friends had an outside lunch at Browning's on Jackson and Main. There, David opened some of his ordination gifts. My table was filled with lively but relaxing conversation thanks to the presence of Fr. Tom Watkins, Fr. Bill Martin, the Kochies and myself.

We got back to Motel 6 around 4:00 p.m. and I stayed in for the evening and watched *The Angel* on TV and read most of *How to Write the Story of Your Life*, an excellent and inspiring book.

David's First Mass of Thanksgiving is at 2:00 p.m. today. I'm looking forward to the great honor of preaching about Matthew's call to follow Christ and how this ties into David's call to journey as a diocesan priest.

June 10, 2002 – Monday
Wake Forest, N.C. – 6:30 p.m.
Sunny – 95 F

David's First Mass of Thanksgiving was a very moving experience. Though it took place at the Mass in Spanish, I think there were as many Anglos as Hispanics there. There was standing room only. We were all very glad that it was a sunny, if hot, day.

One of the best things that happened is that Fr. Daniel Robles finally arrived from Missouri. He had car problems on Saturday, so he missed the ordination. Daniel is a kindred spirit of David and mine, a free spirit who is thoroughly in love with life and filled with humor.

I got lots of laughs from the assembly with my homily, and the people applauded when I was finished. I got many compliments from the priests and guests.

We had a reception in the St. Rita's parish hall after Mass, and there was plenty of Puerto Rican food and dancing. David was having a great old time dancing when Fr. Tom and I had to leave with the Kochies for the airport.

I was exhausted by the time I got home around 11:30 last evening, and today, I was a little on the cranky side at work.

Today, I went to see Rev. John Hartman, pastor of Wake Forest Presbyterian Church. He will be the preacher for the ecumenical vespers service that St. Catherine's is hosting in July. John is a wonderful guy. I'm not surprised his congregation is growing so well.

I also decided today that I would offer two Speaker's Series for adult education during the 2002-2003 academic year at St. Catherine's. The first will be a six-part series called, Documents of Vatican II in the fall. It will feature six documents of the Council that are especially relevant for today: *Sacrosanctum Concilium* (The Constitution on the Sacred Liturgy); *Lumen Gentium* (Dogmatic Constitution on the Church), *Unitatis Redin-*

tegratio (Decree on Ecumenism); *Dei Verbum* (Dogmatic Constitution on Divine Revelation); *Gaudium et Spes* (Pastoral Constitution on the Church in the Modern World); and *Actuositatem* (Decree on the Apostolate of Lay People).

In the spring of 2003, I will offer a five-part series titled *Adventures in American Catholic Spirituality*. I'm not sure which spiritual writers will be featured, but I will definitely include the late Trappist monk, Thomas Merton, and the late Fr. Henri Nouwen. I am also thinking of discussing the spirituality of the four American women martyrs of El Salvador. I'm looking forward to putting both of these series together.

June 11, 2002 – Tuesday – St. Barnabas
Wake Forest, N.C. – 5:45 p.m.
Sunny – 95 F

I think Dorothy Day would make a good person for my *Adventures in American Catholic Spirituality* series. She was a dynamic activist who had a passion for the underdog of society, a true pioneer who fought for the "preferential option of the poor."

This morning, I visited the Dean at Our Lady of Lourdes. It was my annual visit to get our parish records checked and the annual dean's report approved. Interestingly, we had 170 baptisms this past year at St. Catherine's.

I also visited the bishop to have him sign a "recombination" agreement. It's a legal document that formally erases an imaginary line between two pieces of property upon which I want to build the rectory. The bishop seems preoccupied as he gets prepared to travel to Dallas for the meeting of the American bishops. I told him not to get shot as we saw happen yesterday at the Benedictine monastery at Conception, Missouri when a gunman killed two monks and then himself. What a crazy world we live in!

This evening, the finance council will approve the annual budgets for the school and parish. The world situation seems so "iffy" at the present that many people are hanging on to their money more tightly than usual it seems. Just about every parish is having a decrease in offertory.

June 17, 2002 – Monday
Wake Forest, N.C. – 7:30 p.m.
Partly Cloudy – 86 F

The 100-degree weather of last week has finally ended, and we are now in the high 80s. The area is bone dry, and all the grass is brown. We keep hearing that we may get an isolated thunderstorm, but so far the clouds float right on past us. The weather forecast for the next week shows no rain.

The American bishops have concluded their semi-annual meeting in Dallas, and they adopted an interesting policy regarding priests who have sexually abused minors. They will be removed from priestly ministry permanently, but they will not necessarily be thrown out of the priesthood. I think the bishops caved in to the mass media. Things should be decided case by case, I believe, especially in isolated instances that happened many years earlier. I can imagine an alcoholic priest who might have had sex with a minor in his drinking days, but who would not even think of such a thing in sobriety. There seems to be little Christian mercy in the bishops' policy, but I am glad that they are not automatically kicking priests out of the priesthood. Perhaps this will begin the healing process.

Last evening, I had a wonderful phone conversation with Fr. Steve Worsley, who will be the next Vicar for Priests. He is a delightful person and very sharp. In his life before priesthood, he was a pediatrician. We talked about the priesthood and the things that I have found helpful. I shared with him how I arranged one on one lunches with pastors whom I admire so that I could learn from them. This has been sort of a self-designed independent study course I created for myself. Steve thinks this might be a good journal article, and I think he may have a good idea. I'll begin putting together some notes about this idea.

The only bad thing in my life right now is the sale of the five acres of land that certain developers want St. Catherine's to buy. Last week, they wrote a very ugly letter to our diocesan attorney claiming that I did not support the sale aggressively enough and that they might sue me. They suggested that the diocese should give them an extension to make up for my lack of enthusiasm for selling the land.

Therefore, on Thursday, I met with our diocesan attorney and chancellor. We decided to grant the builder a two-month extension to obtain the city's approval, on the condition that they would drop any threat to sue me. Today, they sent a letter saying that they would agree not to sue me if the bishop and I would support the project and if neither of us would interact with "appointed or elected officials" of Wake Forest. Then, they had the gall to ask for an additional extension until December 30th of this year instead of August 30th! On top of that, they wrote a flowery letter that is supposed to come from the Diocese of Raleigh. I'll answer tomorrow or a few days from now. The potential buyers are counting on the neighbors to cool off from their opposition to the land sale. Hell will freeze over first, I think!

June 22, 2002 – Saturday
Wake Forest, N.C. – 8:30 a.m.
Cloudy – 85 F

I have a great sense of internal peace this Saturday morning. Things seem to be going well for me, and summer is a slower time in my parish. With the school kids out for the summer, and with no Faith Formation classes for the youth, things seem quieter. It's a great time to work on projects that we have not had time to do during the year.

On Thursday, Fr. Bill Pitts, head of our diocesan Society for the Propagation of the Faith, treated the Diocese of Raleigh staff and me to lunch at the Macaroni Grill in Cary, N.C. This was to celebrate the winning of the Archbishop O'Meara First Place award from the Catholic Press Association. The award was given to Fr. Pitts, NC *Catholic*, and to me as writer of the series I did on my Ugandan adventures. I am now preparing the series for market, and I plan on sending the series to *Catholic Digest* next week.

Yesterday, I had lunch with Sr. Betty Bullen, Pastoral Administrator of Our Lady of the Rosary (OLR) Parish in Louisburg, N.C. As supervising pastor of the daughter parish of St. Catherine's, I like to keep abreast of what is happening there. OLR is growing very slowly, but it is growing. The parish is hoping to buy an older house for Sr. Betty, a house they found for $82,000. It needs some work, but the parish has plenty of volunteers to work on it. Sr. Betty also reported on a very successful father-son campout on the parish land a couple of weeks ago. Fr. Brien, a Dominican who has done lots of work in San Pedro Sula, Honduras, has been offering Mass in Spanish once a month and has helped the community in other ways. I am very grateful for that.

My parish continues to grow like a weed as does Wake Forest. Today's *Raleigh News & Observer* reported that the town is getting five new grocery stores including the state's first Super Target store. Next month, I-540 will open to Capital Blvd., and in August, the new Triangle Town Center, a 1.3 million acre shopping mall, will open right by Capital Blvd. and I-540. The town should really begin exploding with those developments as I-540 and the new mall are only seven miles down the road from us.

On July 1st, Bonson Hobson, chief of WKWW Architects, will come to St. Catherine's to see our place. That is the firm that is going to do a site plan for the parish, designing where all of our wish list buildings and fields and parking lots will be located. I am eager to meet Bonson and to begin the design process. I think once we have a site plan on paper, the people of the parish will get excited.

The other day, I also talked with Msgr. Casto Adeti, Vicar General of Arua Diocese in Uganda. He is doing mission appeals in the Pittsburgh area where his brother is working on his Ph.D. at Duquesne University. Msgr. Adeti was a most gracious host to me when I went to Arua Diocese last year, and he visited my parish last summer. With the money St. Catherine's raised for him in a second collection—about $7,800—the Diocese of Arua was able to buy many bicycles for catechists who have to travel to distant chapels on terrible roads. That diocese also gave $500 to each of three parishes that I visited. I still get letters and photos from the pastors of the parishes I visited.

This coming Tuesday morning, I will be having breakfast with one or two of our Maryknoll Affiliates who will be going to Uganda in the fall. I am hoping that they might want to go to visit Arua while they are in Uganda. Arua, for the most part, has not yet gotten electricity, so it is one of the poorest of the 19 Ugandan dioceses.

June 26, 2002 – Wednesday
Wake Forest, N.C. – 6:00 p.m.
Cloudy with slight rain

Well, we finally got a little rain today, even if it was only about five minutes worth. Perhaps this will break the spell of dryness we have been having. I'm very glad about the rain as is everyone around here.

Forest fires continue to rage in Arizona and Colorado, while some of the Midwest suffers from flooding. The Middle East is still a tinderbox, and President Bush wants Arafat to be removed as head of the Palestinians before giving his blessing for a Palestinian state.

Today, I talked with the Chancellor of the Diocese of Raleigh and the diocesan attorney, Charlie Powers. We agreed that we would let the men who want part of our property have an extension on the land deal until September 30th, but only on the condition that they promise they will not sue the diocese or me. In other words, we are granting the request for an extension based on the fear that they will deliberately try to harm me and the parish.

Fortunately, I had an off-the-record meeting with a very influential person yesterday at my office, and he is squarely on our side. He hopes the land deal will fall through. He mentioned that one of the men on the Wake Forest Planning Board got confused in his voting, and he voted to approve the rezoning of the land when he actually was against the rezoning (which I am also).

Msgr. Casto Adeti of the Diocese of Arua, called me the other day to say hello. I'm going to call him later this evening to see if I can arrange to have our two Maryknoll Affiliates visit a couple of the parishes that I visited in his diocese while they are in Uganda in October. I know they would love to visit the Arua Diocese, one of the poorest in a desperately poor country. If the people are just half as welcoming to the Maryknoll Affiliates as they were to me, I'll be thrilled.

June 27, 2002 – 9:10 p.m.
Wake Forest, N.C.
Rainy – 90 F

Happy Anniversary to me! It was four years ago that Bishop Gossman ordained "The Magnificent Seven" at St. Michael the Archangel Church in Cary, N.C. In one sense, the time has flown by. On the other hand, it feels as though I have been a priest for at least 10 years! That is because God has blessed me with so many experiences in priesthood at St. Mark's in Wilmington and now here at St. Catherine's in Wake Forest. Plus, I have had many wonderful experiences teaching sociology at the University of North Carolina at Wilmington and then for a year at NC State University, and my missionary trips to Guatemala, El Salvador, Honduras and Uganda. I love being a priest! I can't think of anything more fulfilling and suited for me.

Today was pretty much routine—many different things to deal with. Two of the staff and I went to Applebee's for lunch, a new restaurant in our town. That was my special anniversary treat to myself.

Today, the U.S. Supreme Court ruled that vouchers for private, including Catholic, schools were legal. The case came from my hometown, Cleveland, which is very Catholic. I don't know what effect this will have on our own Catholic schools in the Diocese of Raleigh. Perhaps it will help more poor students come to St. Catherine's who cannot afford the tuition.

A young man came to my office this evening. He is suffering from Bipolar Affective Disorder. He has written a screenplay that has caught the eye of a major Hollywood studio and at least one nationally known director. My task is to help him get legal help right away before he screws up the deal with his hypomania.

June 29, 2002 – Saturday – SS Peter & Paul
Morehead City, N.C. - 2:45 p.m.
Partly cloudy – 85 F

I had a very pleasant journey to the coast this morning. St. Egbert's is 160 miles from my house. I dropped over to Atlantic City, N.C. before coming to the rectory to buy Fr. Charles a bathing suit and beach towel for when he comes to visit in September from Africa. I will take him to our annual diocesan priest retreat at the ocean the first week he arrives.

My whole journey to Morehead City was filled with thinking of a visit I had on Thursday evening after Mass, the fourth anniversary of my ordination. The visit was from a woman who wants to start a rightwing chapter of women at my parish. I know very little about the group except that it is affiliated with a religious group noted for being one of the most conservative—or reactionary—groups in Catholicism. Our Diocese has had some problems with this group in the past, and vocation directors from all over the country universally warn others to keep this community out of their dioceses.

I gave the women permission to spend an hour in front of the Blessed Sacrament once a month. How could I refuse to let parishioners worship the Lord! I also let them have a room in which to meet each Tuesday evening. I made it clear that they would not be an official group of the parish and that they are to have no contact with children or youth of our parish, outside of their own.

I am very conflicted about the group. I hate the severe negativity that rightwing groups often exhibit. On the other hand, I feel I must be open and nurturing to their spiritual journeys. After all, how could I fault prayer, sharing of self, community and visits to the Blessed Sacrament?

I will seek the advice of pastors in the Raleigh Deanery that I trust and I will do plenty of praying.

Last evening, I went to the first meeting of our St. Catherine Marriage Prep Team. It is a great group of people, and we had a fine dinner of ham and turkey.

When I got to Morehead City, N.C., I spent some time talking with Sean Chapman, a seminarian of St. Mary's in Baltimore who is at St. Egbert's doing his summer assignment before taking a summer vacation and then going to his annual seminarian beach retreat on Emerald Isle, N.C. I'll take him out to dinner after the two Saturday Masses. It's nice to hear a seminarian's views, concerns and struggles. I must do more for vocation awareness at St. Catherine's and for seminarians!

JULY 2002

July 1, 2002 – Monday
Wake Forest, N.C. – 8:30 p.m.
94 F – Sunny to partly cloudy

The weekend at St. Egbert's went very well. It was great to get out of town and get a fresh perspective on things. The people of St. Egbert's were very receptive to my mission appeal. I preached about St. Catherine's two sister parishes in San Pedro Sula, Honduras and Muduuma, Uganda and our efforts to help them.

One family with three children stopped me after one of the Masses. The mom told me that her three children, totally on their own, decided to give all the money they had saved for an outing that day for St. Catherine's missionary works.

After the fifth and final Mass of the weekend, I ran into a teenager named Kristin and her mom. After talking a bit, they told me how much they wish they could have a Maryknoll Affiliate chapter there at St. Egbert's. Kristin told me she reads *Maryknoll Magazine* every month from cover to cover. As we were talking, another woman came over and said she overheard us and that she too is very interested in an Affiliate chapter. I said I'd drop the pastor, Fr. Greg, a note about it. Today, I sent an email to Maryknoll Sister Janet who is national head of the Maryknoll Affiliates. Who knows, perhaps we will have another North Carolina chapter! That would be the third one I have started.

Today was very special in the history of St. Catherine's. Business Manager Gael Gormaly and I met with Bonson Hobson, head of WKWW Architects from Charlotte. His agency will be doing the site plan for our campus. After touring the campus, we had lunch at Applebee's. He seems to be a very likeable man with plenty of experience building churches. We talked about the concept of balconies, and he shared with us a plan he's doing in Burlington, N.C. that includes balconies on both sides. He said that that is the cheapest way to build seating in a sanctuary. We also discussed the possibility of having classrooms for Faith Development underneath the main sanctuary.

July 2, 2002 – Tuesday
Wake Forest, N.C. – 95 F
Sunny with light rain

I began this morning by meeting with a man named George at his home in an older part of Wake Forest that I had never been to before. He was there with his son and daughter-in-law. I was there to celebrate the Sacrament of the Sick with George as he is having surgery at the Durham VA Medical Center on July 15th. He is having a kidney removed, and he is pretty sure he won't make it. The physicians told him that with the procedure he will have, even a 20-year-old would have a difficult time surviving.

George met with the local funeral home the other day—the undertaker—and talked about arrangements. The funeral director wanted to know if he wanted the service to be at the funeral home or at the church, and George figured the funeral home would do. I suggested he have a wake service at the funeral home in the evening and then a funeral Mass at St. Catherine's. He loved it when I said, "George, why not go out in style? I'll do you proud." So, he'll probably have "the works" should the time come, and our Comfort Committee will have a luncheon for his family. But as I pointed out to George, he may pull through just fine.

This was an interesting visit for me because just the other week I met with a woman who was making arrangements in advance in case her husband dies soon. That man also was a patient at the Durham VA Medical Center. The woman was beside herself with joy to learn that I would be happy to have a funeral Mass for her Lutheran husband.

After visiting George, I visited two delightful parishioners who have been with the parish for many, many years. Tommy is a former New York Yankees pitcher, and his wife, Sue is celebrating her birthday today. I love parishioners like Tommy and Sue—down to earth, no hyper-religiosity, no phony baloney—just good, plain Christian folks. How refreshing.

This afternoon, I went to the Wake Forest Ministerial Association meeting and welcomed Rev. Gayla Collins, new pastor of the Wake Forest United Methodist Church, into our community. Gayla was there with her minister husband. She seems like a fine person and will probably make a valuable new member of the clergy community of our town.

My fine day went well until a woman was "possessed by the Holy Spirit" and would not get up from lying prostrate on the floor of the sanctuary. I finally got her up, but I was tempted to call the police at one point. I must admit that I do live an interesting life!

July 3, 2002 – Wednesday – St. Thomas the Apostle
Wake Forest, N.C. – 9:00 p.m.
Partly cloudy – 95 F

Today, I had my annual eye exam. This year, I went to a new group of optometrists and had a delightful young O.D. named Dr. Yokum. He said that he had heard good things about me, and one of my parishioners used to work with him. We hit it off well. I'll get some new glasses on Monday.

Today, I learned that a young Mexican woman who was planning on getting married this Saturday at St. Catherine's has been unable to get a marriage license. Because she is in the country illegally, it is very difficult. I'm sorry for her and her young fiancé, as I baptized them at the Easter Vigil Mass, and recently had the privilege of confirming them and giving them their First Holy Communion. Unfortunately, the young woman, who is in her late teens, is pregnant with her first child. The non-bride and non-groom are going ahead with their fiesta anyway since the invitations have been sent. I understand the "bride" will dress up in her wedding gown. I hope they have a great party.

Today, the workers broke a gas line on the St. Catherine campus, so the staff went home early. Because our staff takes responsibility so seriously, I didn't even have to go to the campus on this day off.

July 6, 2002 – Saturday
Wake Forest, N.C. – 7:25 a.m.
Sunny – 90 F

Yesterday, the temperature got up to 100 degrees in the area, but today it is supposed to be a bit cooler. We had a few drops of rain, but the drought continues. The little dogwood tree in my front yard is pretty much dead due to the drought and some disease it caught. The flowers in the front yard struggle with the heat, and I need to water them each day.

Yesterday, the new vicar for priests, Fr. Steve Worsley, sent me an email asking if I would come to one of the new priests' meetings he is hosting. My job would be twofold: first, discuss how to maintain healthy boundaries in the priests' professional and personal lives and, second, discuss the idea of "understanding the pastor's point of view." Needless to say, I am delighted to be of help.

This weekend, I am working on our Parish Plan – 2002-2003. It was due on July 1st to the diocese, but because of other things our parish has been working on, mostly our self-study, we were not able to get around to it until now. I hope to send it off next week.

I received a nice email from a priest friend who is on an extended retreat in Canada. He is working on many personal issues in his life and learning more and more about himself.

This past week, the priests of the Diocese of Raleigh received a sneak preview of an upcoming article to be published in the next issue of the *NC Catholic*. It discusses the grave financial problems that a Cape Fear Deanery parish is facing. Apparently, there has been poor stewardship for the past couple of years. How the problem will be solved is unknown. I hope the diocese does not assess every parish some money to make up the debt of that parish.

July 7, 2002 – 14th Sunday in Ordinary Time
Wake Forest, N.C. – 7:00 p.m.
Sunny – 90 F

This weekend, I officiated at a very nice wedding, three baptisms, and the usual five Masses. Though I'm pretty worn out by the end of the Masses on Sunday, this parish fills me with incredible joy and excitement!

Today, I preached on how we can turn our worries and concerns over to Jesus, and He will give us rest. I told the story of Babe Ruth and how much at peace he was following a visit with a priest the night before his surgery in December 1946. I told how often I carry around the weight of the world on my shoulders and then, when the load finally gets too heavy for me, I turn it over to God. Immediately, I get a sense of relief. Why I don't turn over my problems earlier, I don't know.

I also talked about the concept of "packaging" that I learned from nursing. An example of packaging might be a patient who turns his call light on 47 times in an eight hour period. Assuming the patient is not desperately ill, this is obviously not acceptable, for the nurse could not get his or her work done. Thus, we "package" the patient's requests. For example, we might design a care plan that says the nurse will visit the patient on the hour for five minutes, but no more. The example I used of packaging today was that of putting my worries in an imaginary package and then deciding that I would deal with them at a particular time. For example, rather than worry constantly throughout the day about a problem, I might say, "Okay, I'll schedule a 'worry session' from 10:00-10:15 a.m. tomorrow. I won't worry at other times." It's amazing how this practical tip works. I challenged the people to try it out and let me know how it works.

I just finished designing the 2002-2003 Parish Plan goals and objectives for our parish. The goals are seven:

1. The offertory will increase by 25% by June, 2013;
2. The parish will have a new master plan for future building by March, 2013;
3. The parish will have six new outdoor structures by June, 2004;
4. The parish will raise $2,000,000 in gifts and pledges towards its new sanctuary and office complex during the fiscal years from 2002-2004;
5. The Faith Development Department (FDD) will at least double the number of offerings for adult faith formation during the 2002-2003 fiscal year;
6. St. Catherine of Siena Catholic School will increase its enrollment by 100 students form 2002-2004;
7. The St. Catherine of Siena Vocation Department will design a parish-wide blueprint for vocation development n the 2002-2003 fiscal year.

I think that is plenty to work on for now, and this does not include all the work we are doing in the area of missions, Hispanic ministry and other things! But I have no doubt that God will continue to shower us with blessings so that we will be successful.

July 8, 2002 – Monday
Wake Forest, N.C. – 9:00 p.m.
Sunny day – 90 F

I went to Amazon.com the other day looking to see what's new in the world of qualitative research books as I want to be up to date to be a good consultant for the Duke University School of Nursing. I was amazed to find that in the past 10 years while I have been in the seminary and priesthood, there have been several books written not just in qualitative research methods, but also in qualitative research methods in nursing.

I was wondering what books might and might not be good when I saw in the newspaper this morning a blurb about a nursing professor at UNC-Chapel Hill, Margarete Sandelowski. It seems that Professor Sandelowski has been named the Cary C. Boshamer distinguished professor of nursing and that she is an expert in qualitative research methods. I will call her tomorrow to see if I can get an appointment and pick her brain about what's good and what's not.

On the parish front, Principal Ed came to my office this afternoon to say that it is possible that all but one student of the third grade class may be going to another school. That has always been a very small class. The fourth grade class has only nine students. As I see it, the only thing we can do is combine the two classes even though not many people like such an arrangement. There is no way to financially justify having a third grade teacher for just one to four kids. We'll try to have a meeting this Thursday with third and fourth grade parents and let them know our dilemma.

This afternoon, I had lunch with a priest at El Sombrero in Zebulon, N.C. We had a very nice chat and he turned me on to Celebrity Cruise Line that gives priests free passage for celebrating Mass once per day. Otherwise, the priest is free to enjoy the cruise. He may take a guest for free on the trip. I will have to explore this.

Today, I received Andrew M. Greeley's *My Love: A Prayer Journal*. I love reading Andy's prayer journals. I also look forward to reading his latest novel that I received the other day, *The Bishop in the West Wing*.

July 11, 2002 – Thursday – St. Benedict
Wake Forest, N.C. – 9:00 p.m.
Rain off and on – cloudy – 80s F

What a difference a day makes! Yesterday was my day off, and I had a very relaxing time. I got a new pair of glasses, went grocery shopping, read a screen play called *Manic Ride* written by one of my parishioners, had my usual Wednesday private Mass at my dining room table and watched TV.

Today was one thing after another! Among other things, I learned that the Wake Forest Planning Board approved the rezoning of the five acres that I really don't want to sell. That means that it will only take a simple majority of 3-2, instead of a 4-1 vote, of the Town Council to approve the rezoning. Well, I figure it is now in God's hands. Whatever happens will be His will. During the day, different staff talked to me about problems with other staff. The things they told me were nothing I have not heard before.

This evening, the third and fourth grade parents met. Because of the small numbers, we have to combine the two classes. The parents shared their concerns, but the meeting went very positively. I think everyone left with the idea that all will be well.

July 12, 2002 – Friday
Wake Forest, N.C. – 8:00 p.m.
Sunny – low 80s F

Today, some of us spent a couple of hours cleaning up our building, moving school desks, chairs, books, computers, tables and other paraphernalia out of the hallways and into rooms to make the building more presentable for the events we are hosting next week. On Tuesday, we are hosting the Wake Forest Ecumenical Vespers Service and on Thursday, we are hosting a Chamber of Commerce event called "Business After Hours."

Among the ministers coming to the vespers service are those from the Wake Forest Baptist Church, Friendship Chapel Baptist Church, Wake Forest Presbyterian Church, Wake Forest United Methodist Church, and the Ridgecrest Baptist Church. The Lutheran minister is unable to come and the Episcopal clergy does not seem to be into ecumenism.

The building looks great now. Perhaps the floors of our new Trinity Center will be ready by Monday so that we can move most of the school desks and such into those classrooms.

July 14, 2002 – Sunday
Wake Forest, N.C. – 7:10 p.m.
Sunny – 80s F

I just love this parish! I get so incredibly energized each weekend celebrating liturgy and meeting all the folks.

This weekend, I told one of my favorite stories from "The Flats" section of Cleveland, Ohio. It was about a little boy who received a donut and milk from the pastor of St. Malachi's Church on the Lower West Side of Cleveland. The priest told him that he should always feel free to come to St. Malachi's whenever he was hungry and that there would always be a donut and milk for him. The little boy said, "I was afraid to come here today, Father, because I'm not Catholic." The wise priest smiled and said, "That's okay, because our doughnuts aren't Catholic either."

Some years later, a young man came to St. Malachi's and a friend of mine—Sr. Donna Marie—was on duty. He had brought several trays of exquisite food for the poor from a fancy restaurant in The Flats. He went on to explain how several years earlier, before The Flats had become a ritzy place with fancy restaurants and nightclubs, he had come to St. Malachi's with his friend. He told about how the priest reassured him that not being Catholic was okay, for the doughnuts weren't Catholic either. And he told the sister that when he was a boy, often the doughnut and milk he had gotten from St. Malachi's was the only food he had before going to school. And he vowed that someday, he would come back to St. Malachi's to return the favor. Now was the time. The good seeds of compassion that the priest had planted fell into the good soil of the little boy, and they flourished. Now they produced seed for others.

After reflecting on this story, I contacted Sr. Donna Marie by email and asked her if she would be interested in sharing some of her great ministry ideas with us via an educational retreat. She has years of experience and has gathered some of the most brilliant and successful forms of ministry. It would be a shame to ignore such a treasure trove of ministerial ideas.

Today, I finally learned how to use the cell phone that I have had for several months! Now, when I go to Ohio a week from tomorrow, I can take it along with me and use it in case I have an accident.

On Saturday, we had a Salvadoran wedding at St. Catherine's followed by three baptisms in which I used water from the River Jordan. This morning, someone from the 7:30 a.m. Mass crowd turned in two $100 bills to me that he found in the parking lot. Nobody at the 7:30 a.m. Mass claimed them, and then I had a hunch that they might belong to the groom from the day before. Sure enough, the new groom was cleaning the dining room with his friends and was thrilled that his $200 had been found. What a great parish this is!

The coming week will be filled with writing Vol. 1, No. 2 of our parish's Building & Finance News, two Pastor's Corners and two homilies—which I just finished. Now, I have to write out the homilies for Spanish translation.

July 15, 2002 – Monday – St. Bonaventure
Wake Forest, N.C. – 11:00 p.m.
Mostly sunny day – 90 F and very humid

It turned out to be a great day. The building is sparkling in preparation for our Wake Forest Ecumenical Vespers Service tomorrow and the "Business After Hours" celebration on Thursday. The Ladies' Guild is getting ready to put on a spread for the Vespers Service guests, and four of the school children will wear their uniforms and hand out programs to the guests.

At noon, I went to Henderson, N.C. to bless the house of some Mexicans. I was happy to do so. Not only did I get to see the whole family in their environment, it was the first time I had ever been to Henderson, which is north of Wake Forest on US-1. Even though the Catholic Church in Henderson has a Mass in Spanish each week, many of the Spanish-speaking people travel the almost 30 miles to St. Catherine's each Sunday.

This evening, I spent some time with a new parishioner named Jesús. He is a man perhaps in his 40s. He is a second-generation bilingual Puerto Rican man who is a retired Army Lt. Colonel. I believe he will be an excellent leader in the Hispanic community of St. Catherine's. He will help Sergio and Rosa translating my homilies, so each one would have to translate only every third week. Jesús also wants to work with youth ministry in the Hispanic community. Youth ministry is something that we do not do well in the Hispanic community, so I'm pinning a lot of hope on Jesús. He is also seriously considering becoming a deacon. Jesús said he looked at many area Catholic churches and found St. Catherine's to be best suited for him. What a wonderful place St. Catherine's is thanks to a God who continues to shower blessings on us so very abundantly!

July 16, 2002 – Tuesday – OL Mt. Carmel
Wake Forest, N.C. – 4:45 p.m.
Sunny – 95 F and humid

I had a wonderful visit this morning with Fr. Bob Curry, S.J., my spiritual director. He will be leaving at the end of September, as his time will be up as Pastor of St. Raphael's. We had a nice chat about my plan for working to solve a problem with right-wingers who seem to be trying to make St. Catherine's their base of operation.

I just talked with my friend, Fr. Ed Holland. He's a Parochial Vicar of Holy Family parish in Parma, Ohio. We're going to get together on Thursday the 25th for lunch. It'll be great to hear about all the news in the Cleveland Diocese—and I know there is plenty!

I just got an email from a dear friend of mine, Dr. Pam Brink, Editor of the *Western Journal of Nursing Research*. I had written her this morning about how the older I get, the more I am convinced that simplicity and clarity are supreme values for the good scholar and writer. The truly excellent scholar, like the truly good writer, is able to take the complex and present it in a clear and simple manner. Pam took my "two-cents' worth" of philosophy and is using it for an editorial in the *WJNR*. I'm flattered. This is the second time I've been in an editorial for that journal. Once, I was in there talking about how it is important to never let one's job get in the way of one's career. The two are very different concepts. The former puts food on the table. The other is your true identity peg that nurtures your spirit. Pam and I used to teach together at The University of Iowa. Such treasured memories!

I'm getting excited for this evening's Wake Forest Ecumenical Vespers Service. I hope it all goes well and that it touches some hearts.

July 17, 2002 – Wednesday
Wake Forest, N.C. – 7:00 a.m.
Sunny – 98 F

The Ecumenical Service went very well last night. The music provided by our two bands and the food were super, and the homily that Rev. John Hartman gave was great. There were about 300 people attending. It was nice to get the various ministers together and introduce the new pastor of the Wake Forest United Methodist Church, Rev. Gayla Collins. In addition to Gayla and Rev. Hartman, Pastor of the Wake Forest Presbyterian Church, we had Dr. Enoch Holloway, Pastor of Friendship Chapel Baptist Church (our biggest African-American congregation), Dr. Tom Jackson, Pastor of the Wake Forest Baptist Church, and Rev. Larry Ogle, Pastor of Ridgecrest Baptist Church. Alma Anides read the Gospel in Spanish.

While we were worshiping the Lord, the Town Council was voting on the fate of the five acres of land that developers want to buy from St. Catherine's. After our service, while we were all in the dining room enjoying food and fellowship, one of the members of our congregation came to report that the Town Council voted 3-2 to rezone the five acres so construction of town homes could be built. However, because 100 percent of the homeowners in the area signed a petition to oppose the project, the measure failed as it would have taken a vote of 4-1 to approve the land sale.

I do not know if the developers will try something else in August or September. They have until September 30th to get their plans through the

Town Council. I put nothing past this crowd! The Town Council got the developers to reduce their wish list of 40 town homes down to 34 and then down to 29. The developer said that less than 29 would not be cost effective.

If the developers give up now, we will have these precious five acres of land. This, I believe, would be best for our parish community in the long run. On the other hand, if the developers eventually get their way with the Town Council and we are forced to sell these five acres, we will get $250,000 that can be put towards our new sanctuary. Either way, we win. It is totally in God's hands right now, so whatever happens, I am seeing it as God's will.

July 19, 2002 – Friday
Wake Forest, N.C. – 7:10 p.m.
Partly Sunny – 95 F

The last two days have been very interesting. Yesterday, I had a delightful time with George, an older man who has metastatic cancer. He has spent his whole life working in steel, and he also was very active in his parish and in scouting. He is a "salt-of-the-earth" type. We also talked about the pain he feels from losing his wife of 56 years a year ago. He reminded me a great deal of my paternal grandfather— a simple, humble, giving man who lives his vocation hidden from most of humanity.

In the past two days, I have been helping the principal try to cope with a group of parents who have left the school, and I have met with some parents who came to talk with me about their decision to leave the school because they are moving or because they cannot handle the negativity of gossip. This makes me weary because as pastor, I have so much on my plate already. It is a joy to know that strong and competent people are heading parish ministries. When there is a ministry head who is not inspiring confidence, it takes me away from my own work. I'll live. And I will also be supervising the school leadership much more closely in the coming academic year.

Last evening, Kathleen Varner, our development director, headed up "Business After Hours" for the Wake Forest Chamber of Commerce. It was a resounding success. We had a wonderful spread of food in the din-ing room, and people took tours of the new Trinity Center. I met many interesting people. Borders' Restaurant provided some delicious food for the event, just as La Foresta had supplied meatballs for the Tuesday Vesper Service event. Parishioners love to contribute to the parish. God bless them!

I also learned from one of the Town Council members that the battle over the five-acre plot of land is probably over. That is because the people who want to buy the land cannot bring the project up to the Town Coun-cil for six months. Because our contract says that after September 30th we no longer have to sell the property, it appears we have the land for good. Though we will miss the $250,000 that we would have obtained from such a sale, in the long run, the parish will benefit from having this land. I am very pleased.

Today, I had an interesting meeting with the leader of the home-school parents. They have agreed that they would like to be an official group of the parish. I told them they would have to agree to use the Dio-cese of Raleigh religious education materials and to be directly supervised by the diocese and myself. They agreed to that. However, I have noted that at least three of the eight mothers in the group are members of a lay religious group noted for operating in a parallel church kind of way. For purposes of this journal, I will call the group "PC." I told the leader of the home-school group, who is also the spokesperson for the PC group, that I wanted the list of names for the home-school parents and the PC group that is meeting at St. Catherine's.

I also told the home-school leader that I was checking in with other pastors in the area about the consequences of having a group such as theirs meeting on campus, even if it is not an official part of the parish. I told the home-school leader that PC, and priest affiliate—which I'll call "MC" for purposes of this journal—are extremely controversial. Because I am a new priest and one who is not experienced in dealing with such phenomena on a parish level, I have to seek the advice of other pastors and sociologists. I know at least two pastors who have had terrible, terrible experiences with MC and its related groups. I want St. Catherine's to be a solid, loving, middle-of-the-road post-Vatican II congregation, not a haven for highly controversial groups who often divide communities.

I offered Mass this morning for a special intention, that the Holy Spirit would guide me to do the right thing for the people of PC who are my parishioners and also for the parish as a whole. The Holy Spirit will guide me, I have no doubt. Plus, the pastors, from whom I am seeking advice, are one of the ways the Spirit will speak to me.

I later learned that the male PC group that meets at another parish is meeting there under false pretenses. A group of men asked for permission to meet to study a particular book, but they did not let their group's identity be known to the pastor. When the pastor found out the true nature of the group, he told the staff that when the book meeting is over, the PC group would be told that there is no meeting room for them.

Today, Connie, Susanne and I went to Milton's Pizza on Six Forks Road in Raleigh. We received a couple of free passes the other day, so we took advantage of this. It is nice to get out once in a while with the staff members, especially on a Friday afternoon. We also stopped at Staples for some supplies as we each had a $10 off coupon.

I'm looking forward to going to Ohio on Monday! Not only am I looking forward to seeing family and friends, I love the drive up I-77 through Virginia and West Virginia to Ohio. Long drives are my best times for meditation and creative thinking!

July 20, 2002 – Saturday
Wake Forest, N.C. – 6:25 a.m.
Partly cloudy with thunderstorms in the evening – 91 F

Here are a few financial gems by Andrew Tobias that appeared in last week's *Parade* magazine that I'm including here to remember:

- "He is richest who is content with least." – Socrates
- "Buy straw hats in the wintertime. Summer will surely come." – Financier Bernard Baruch
- "Rich people plan for four generations. Poor people plan for Saturday night." – Gloria Steinem
- "The only thing tainted about money is, it 'taint mine or 'taint enough." – An old Georgia governor

- "If you want a kitten, start out by asking for a horse." – attributed on the Internet to Naomi, age 15

Later – 8:20 p.m.

This morning, I did a graveside service for a premature stillborn. The Mexican family named the child after its mother, Rosío. This was the first time I did a graveside service in Spanish. After the ceremony, the funeral director put the little box in the grave, and the men of the group each put at least one shovel filled with dirt on top of the box. When the family men were done doing that, I asked the brother of the dead baby if he would like to "help" me put some dirt in the ground. Naturally, he did, so the two of us put a shovel full of dirt.

Later, I talked with Yves, a woman from St. Raphael's Hispanic community. She was there as the translator for this family who did not speak English. Yves is a leader of the Hispanic community at St. Raphael's, and we enjoyed talking about our two parishes and the needs of the Hispanic communities at both.

Later, I had two baptisms in Spanish, two in English, an hour of Reconciliation and the 5:00 p.m. Mass. This evening, I received a phone call from a missionary friend who has gotten into trouble and now needs special prayers.

July 21, 2002 – 16th Sunday of Ordinary Time
Wake Forest, N.C. – 4:10 p.m.
Sunny – 92 F

I talked to a young man named David today. On Friday, I blessed a container of water for him. When I asked him what the holy water was for, he said he was going to sprinkle his skate hockey team with it as they had a game. Today, I asked him how his team did, and he told me they won. His teammates thanked him for bringing the water along!

It was another beautiful weekend at St. Catherine's. The Hispanic community applauded for me today after one of the leaders told them how cheerful I always am even when very busy.

I told the story of a boy named Eddie who had been left at an orphanage when he was six years old because his mother was unable to care for him. Eddie screamed that he hated her and would never forgive her. Forty years later, just before Eddie was ordained a priest, he called his mother to tell her he loved her and forgave her. A long, tearful, and joyful telephone conversation ensued between son and mother. This story fit in with the idea of mercy that we hear about in today's various Scripture readings. The people seemed to like the homily.

Today, Jesús came to the Mass in Spanish. He hopes to start a thriving youth ministry for our Hispanic kids. That would be a tremendous blessing. Then a young man named Carlos came up to me and asked if there was some community service he could do in the community. When I brought up the idea of helping Jesús with the youth ministry, he seemed very pleased. Carlos is a pretty sharp young man.

I'm looking forward to having a very pleasant and relaxing evening at home, reading the paper, having snacks and watching TV. Then I'll leave for Ohio early tomorrow morning to visit family and friends. I love the trip there and look forward to getting away, even though it's only a few days.

July 24, 2002 – Wednesday
Uniontown, Ohio – 9:00 a.m.
Sunny – 78 F

I'm writing this from my folks' home in Uniontown this morning.

The trip here Monday was great. The weather was terrific. The State of West Virginia is more beautiful in the summer than at any other time of the year, I think. I love driving through the mountains.

Yesterday and today, I celebrated Mass with my parents at the kitchen table. Among other things, we prayed that this house will sell quickly. They are building a condo in Stow, Ohio and they plan to move in mid to late September. This is a beautiful house, and I'm sure they will miss it after 19 years. However, as they get older, they feel it is time to downsize and not have to care for such a large yard. Plus, at the condo, they'll be within a few miles of the homes of my sisters, Chris and Jeanette.

On Monday evening, I went with Dad to see Chris' new house in Cuyahoga Falls, the town where I spent most of my growing up years—6-14 years of age. It is a very spacious home that is plenty big for her four kids and herself. Chris felt that there were too many memories in her other house memories of her late husband, Rich. I blessed the house. It still needs a lawn and landscaping, but Dad and members of Chris' church community, The Chapel in Akron, will help.

Yesterday, I picked up my aunts Olga and Mary in Maple Heights and took them to lunch at the Golden Dragon in Northfield. We got caught up on our lives, their kids and grandkids and my parish. They say I'm part Jewish because so many people want to help me in my ministry—for free. They both walk slowly and with pain. I knew Olga and Mary from the time I was born. Olga eventually married her next door neighbor, my Uncle Norm, and became my aunt. I call Mary my aunt too even though she's not officially that.

In the afternoon, I visited with my Uncle Art who lives in Our Lady of the Angels Parish on the West Side of Cleveland. It's been 14 months since his wife, Ann died. He seems to be getting by, but his walking has slowed down considerably. We got caught up on the family (his kids and grandkids) and then went to dinner at George's Kitchen on Triskett Road. He misses Ann very much. As he says, it is not much fun going places alone.

Later – 4:00 p.m.

This morning, I visited my Aunt Bobbie and Uncle Jim. Bobbie had a very bad illness some months ago, and she's bouncing back slowly. She has lost 25 pounds and is on continuous oxygen. They've been married around 48 years and are hoping to celebrate their 50th anniversary one day. I hope they make it. Bobbie asked Jim, "I wonder if we'll make it to 50."

I then visited my sister Jeanette in Stow and helped her get the family room ready for Mass tomorrow. We'll have a special Mass with her prayer group friends and then have a breakfast. I always enjoy visiting her friends, though theologically they're very conservative and I'm not.

July 25, 2002 – Thursday – St. James
Uniontown, Ohio – 4:00 p.m.
Sunny – 82 F

This morning, I celebrated Mass for Jeanette's prayer group. Lou, one of the men, brought beautiful roses for the altar and flowers for the kitchen table. I offered Mass for the departed husband of one of the women.

I preached on the spirit of giving and talked about the Catholic Church in Uganda. The people loved the red Ugandan chasuble that I wore for this Feast of St. James. There were about 22 people there, and my nephew Steven was the server. After Mass, they took up a collection for Muduuma Parish, St. Catherine's sister parish in Uganda. We raised $107. After the Mass, Jeanette had a huge breakfast for us all.

I then went to Holy Family Parish in Parma to pick up my friend, Fr. Ed Holland. We went out to Carrie Cerino's Ristorante in North Royalton and caught up on each other's life and the latest news of the other priests in the Diocese of Cleveland. Ed was astounded that I have five Masses by myself each weekend as he's in a parish with five priests for 6,000 families. It was great catching up on old times. Ed seems to be doing quite well.

On the way home, I swung into downtown Cleveland and visited the Catholic store on Superior and bought a couple of books and holy cards of St. Catherine of Siena.

July 28, 2002 – 17th Sunday in O.T.
Wake Forest, N.C. – 6:30 p.m.
Sunny – 99 F

It's been a great weekend, filled with wonderful ministerial opportunities.

Yesterday, I had five baptisms, including a baby whose home I blessed the other week. Apparently, my blessing didn't work too well as the women in the house say there is still a ghost who is haunting the place. They didn't tell me there was a ghost there when I went to bless the house. Now, the ghost is scaring one of the kids. I lived in a house in North Liberty, Iowa that was haunted for five years. Then, one day, the ghost disappeared. We talked about how ghosts don't really hurt anyone, but I'm not sure I convinced them.

In the evening, the Welcome Committee had their second welcome dinner for newcomers to the parish. It was a group filled with young couples, some with children and some without—typical St. Catherine crowd.

This weekend, I told the story of the rich nobleman from Scotland who had a simple herdsman named John. Though the nobleman lived in a grand mansion and owned many things, he had no faith and seemed to be owned by his possessions, rather than the other way around. John, on the other hand, lived in a little house with his loving wife and children, was active in his church every Sunday, loved his work and had a house filled with joy.

One day, John came to the nobleman to let him know that he had a dream the night before. In the dream, the Lord told him that the richest man in the valley would die that very day at midnight. Though the nobleman believed neither in God nor in dreams, he became preoccupied. This led him to get a physical exam, which showed he was fine. He also kept the physician with him until five minutes after midnight. When midnight came and passed with him still being alive, he dismissed the physician and went to bed.

At 12:30 a.m., however, John's teenage daughter appeared at the mansion to tell the nobleman that her father had died at midnight. Suddenly, the nobleman realized that although he had all the things money could buy, he was not the richest man in the valley. On the contrary, John had been the richest man in the valley, for he had the treasures that last—love of a family, faith and a good work ethic.

This story led into a discussion about the treasure in the field that Jesus talks about. Things of this world are fleeting, while things of the Kingdom last. I challenged the people to think this week about what they truly treasure.

At the 12:30 p.m. Mass in Spanish, we had a convalidation wedding. It went very well. After the Mass, Sergio said that he overheard at least one couple talking about how they would like to get married also. It seems that many people in the Hispanic community only have a civil wedding that was done in Mexico, but they never got around to having a church wedding. I think perhaps this wedding today might have served as a catalyst that will lead others to convalidate their marriages in the Church.

July 30, 2002 – Tuesday
Wake Forest, N.C. – 10:00 p.m.
Sunny day – 98 F

Life gets more and more interesting for me each passing day!

After visiting my dentist for a postoperative checkup yesterday, I had a great meeting on fundraising. Besides our parish finance director and me, we had the Chancellor and Business Manager of the Diocese of Raleigh, the Assistant Vice President of CCS (a capital campaign firm), and Eric Hector, who is going to head up what we are calling the "in between" capital campaign.

The purpose of this high-powered meeting was to put our parish on a sound journey towards coming up with enough money to build a new sanctuary and office building. The diocesan officials were able to answer some of the questions we had about financing, and Eric Javier of CCS answered some questions about conducting an "in-between" campaign. This campaign is "in-between" the God's Work-Our Challenge (GWOC) campaign and the new big campaign that we will start in fall of 2004. We will be inviting CCS to help us with that, as they did such a great job in helping us with the joint parish/diocesan GWOC campaign.

From this meeting, we decided that the target population for the "in-between" campaign would be the people who are new to the parish since the end of the solicitation period of the GWOC campaign. We will try to raise enough money in pledges to pay off the land we bought. It will be hard to do, but I think that we can do it. I told Erik Hector that I would be very willing to make as many home visits as I possibly can, for we have discovered that people are much more likely to give money asked for by a priest than from lay persons.

Last evening, I did a wake service at Bright's Funeral Home for George M. I enjoyed meeting his family. They are from Pennsylvania originally. Some of them still live there, while others are scattered from Virginia to

Florida. They strike me as real "down home" types of people, much like the people from which I come.

This morning, I did a funeral service for George at the funeral home. Rev. Ned Hill, Pastor of Millbrook United Methodist Church, helped me with the service, as he is the minister of many of George's relatives. Ned brought his assistant minister and a seminarian with him. All three of them are Duke guys. The three men were very bright and cheerful and friendly. I told them that they must have a pretty terrific church if they are the leaders of it.

I then went to visit Mike F., the head of the diocesan schools at the Catholic Center. We're very concerned at the large number of parents who have left the school. We will have a meeting with the principal next week. It's very disconcerting that as the parish keeps growing and growing and growing, the school enrollment is going down.

This evening, I met with a young man who is flying to Los Angeles tomorrow to present his play, *Manic Ride*, to a film company. I am paying for his trip as an investment. Perhaps I'll get a role in the film—wouldn't that be a hoot!

July 31, 2002 – Wednesday – St. Ignatius of Loyola
Wake Forest, N.C. – 7:30 p.m.
Sunny – 94 F

I started off the morning by meeting Bob Neal in the woods on Tyler Run where the new rectory will be built. We marked off the location of the porch, deck and driveway. Bob thinks that perhaps as early as this coming Monday the bulldozers will come to begin clearing the trees for the drive and new home. Very exciting!

Today is the feast of St. Ignatius of Loyola, founder of the Society of Jesus. St. Ignatius is one of my favorite saints, just as the Jesuits are one of my favorite groups of men. One aspect of Ignatius' life that I am most impressed with is his conversion story. After being wounded in battle as a soldier, he was recovering in a castle. He asked for some romance novels to pass the time, but the only books that the castle had were books on the life of Christ and the lives of the saints. God touched Ignatius through the books. Such a story is so very important to people like me, writers who wish to touch lives through their writings.

The other thing that will always make this day very special occurred one year ago today. Our business manager, Gael, and I went to St. Michael the Archangel Parish in Cary. We were taking a tour of all the buildings to get some ideas for St. Catherine's. At the very end of our tour, the administrator-finance person of the parish, Tom Potosky, strongly advised us to try to buy the land next door. We learned that parishes never seem to have enough land to expand. And because so much of our then 20-some acres are not very conducive to building, we took the advice to heart.

From that day in 2001, we set off on a course to buy the 20.5 acres of land next door. After a full year, the land is ours. Now, St. Catherine's has about 43 acres of land on which to grow. I think the purchase of the land is perhaps one of the most significant things I will ever do for the parish historically, at least one of the most significant administrative things. I certainly hope that I will leave a strong mark on the spirituality of the people and tone of this highly energetic and dynamic parish.

AUGUST 2002

August 1, 2002 – Monday – St. Alphonsus Ligouri
Wake Forest, N.C. – 9:40 p.m.
Sunny day – 94 F

Well, here we are in August. This should prove to be a very important month in the life of the parish. It will be especially important for the school, which is having trouble with enrollment. The Tuesday meeting with the principal and head of the diocesan school system should be a milestone in the life of St. Catherine of Siena Catholic School. I pray all goes well with that.

This month, we will also begin a new youth ministry for the Hispanic community and incorporate some new ministers into the Hispanic community. We are currently exploring the possibility of having a parish bulletin printed entirely in Spanish like St. Raphael Parish has. When we called up the company that does our bulletin, they said that St. Raphael's in Raleigh is the only parish in the United States that they service with a wholly Spanish bulletin. We could be the second.

August will also be a good month to prepare lectures, retreats, and new programs. Plus, my good friend Jim from Montana will be coming to visit, so I'll have a few days off later in the month. Perhaps we can go to the Outer Banks for a few days as I have never been there, and Jim would like to see the Outer Banks. Being at the beach is always relaxing for me, and the ocean is a creation that shows the awesomeness of God's power, much like the Rocky Mountains do.

August 2, 2002 – Friday
Wake Forest, N.C. – 8:45 p.m.
Partly cloudy day – 91 F

I had a great lunch with Wray, the head of our Parish Council, today. As I was filling him in all the things we're doing in the parish, it dawned on me just how many things we are doing. Very important things, I might add. The staff and I need to sit down and document all the accomplishments we have made in the second fiscal year I have been at St. Catherine's.

Wray and I also talked about a movie script that we are helping a parishioner get sold. Wouldn't it be a hoot if I got a part in it! I'm investing in the venture but am prepared to get nothing out of the deal except the satisfaction of helping a fellow human being do something highly worthwhile with his life. The whole affair has helped me come up with some terrific plots for future priest novels that I would like to write someday. If I could just ditch TV, I might accomplish something writing-wise!

Speaking of selling things, I just learned that my folks sold their home in Uniontown, Ohio. They'll be moving to a ranch-style condo in Stow, Ohio in September. They'll stay for about a month in my sister Chris' new house. They sold the house within a week after planting a little statue of St. Joseph in the yard.

Today, the staff and I were laughing at the photo of me with a group of First Holy Communion kids. There is a clear halo over my head. I was joking that we should make a clear copy of this, blow it up, and put it on the wall by my office. We could write under it, "Before you start with Fr. Bob, you better know whom you're dealing with!"

August 3, 2002 – Saturday
Wake Forest, N.C. – 8:30 a.m.
Sunny – 94 F

Last Tuesday, July 30th, a teacher by the name of Betty G. Mackie was sentenced to prison for at least eight months for having sex two years ago with a 13-year-old boy, a former student of hers. Mackie, who suffers from bipolar affective disorder, pleaded guilty to the charge on May 22nd.

The judge in the case, Judge Donald W. Stephens, said that if Mackie were a man, she probably would have been charged with a more serious felony that would have called for as much as 20 years in prison (*News & Observer*, Wed., July 31, 2002, p. 10A). It is no surprise to me that a man would receive a much harsher sentence than a woman. This type of sex discrimination is common in America. What surprised me was that the judge admitted such a thing publicly.

What made me very happy was that in yesterday's paper, there were a couple of letters to the editor condemning such anti-male discrimination

(*News & Observer*, Aug. 2, 2002, p. 22A). Today, there was also an excellent letter to the editor (*News & Observer,* Aug. 3, 2002, p. 23A) that reads in part:

> ...as a mother of two boys, something puzzles me. If this had been a great male teacher and a 13-year-old girl in the same circumstances, I think everyone's reaction would have been much stronger.
>
> What are we trying to tell our boys with this reaction? Is it that they are not as important as girls that they should not bother speaking up when something like this happens?
>
> A lot of what I see in the media is "boy negative." I wonder when we will wake up and realize what messages we are giving our boys."
> - C.H., Cary

All I can say is, "Amen!"

August 4, 2002 – 18th Sunday in Ordinary Time
Wake Forest, N.C. – 6:45 p.m.
Sunny – 94 F

What an incredibly interesting weekend! I'm delighted that our Praise & Worship Band, *Soul Purpose*, is back from vacation. The 5:00 p.m. Saturday Mass will now be back to its usual lively celebration.

After that Mass, we had the installation of officers of Council 11234 of the Knights of Columbus. Billy McClain will lead the council for the upcoming year. I envision a great year for this group. It does so very much for the parish despite its relatively small number.

This weekend, I preached on the ministry of the assembly in Eucharist. I told the story of the Pacific island tribe who, when the priest came once a month to celebrate Eucharist, passed around a clump of dirt and grass. This clump symbolized the presence of God in the midst of the community, despite the fact that they were surrounded by water. The exchange of the clump indicated that there was peace and harmony in the village. Only after the clump had made the rounds through the whole community could Eucharist begin. I talked about the duties of the assembly and how they were the Body of Christ. At Eucharist, I said, the "audience" is God. The assembly and priest and other ministers are the actors. Many complimented me later.

Before the 12:30 p.m. Mass, I asked the family of women whose house I had recently blessed how the ghost was doing at their house. I learned that only one girl was having problems. Currently she is unable to sleep. After careful questioning about loss, it turns out that the girl lost both of her grandparents two years ago. She never dealt with it well. Fortunately, she will explore counseling in her community. I will follow.

After this morning's four Masses, two Baptisms and one Presentation, I went to the cemetery outside of Louisburg, N.C. The graveside service was for a 37-year-old Mexican woman, "P." She had a stroke and died after the physicians saved the baby she was carrying. The baby, a little girl, is alive and healthy and weighs just three pounds. She'll be in the hospital for about two months.

The graveside service was very strange. My first clue that something was not quite right was at the moment I entered the cemetery. One of the funeral directors said, in a confidential voice, "Father, this is not a typical family. You'll see." Now, of all the professional people with whom I have dealt with in my life, none can compare with the strict professionalism of funeral directors. They always present themselves with dignity and class. So, for one to make a comment about a family, the family would have to truly be odd.

First of all, we had a Holiness preacher, a Southern Baptist preacher, and me, a Catholic priest. The husband, a Protestant man, came to the proceedings wearing a filthy T-shirt that barely covered his beer-belly, and grungy pants. He was very friendly but rather out of place compared to everyone else who wore more "funeral-like" clothes. Most of the people attending were Hispanics.

Because of the large crowd, most of the people could not fit under the green tent where the casket was resting over the gravesite. The sun was blazing down on us, and the temperature was 94 degrees. First, the Holiness minister said some prayers and a little homily. Then the Baptist minister said a prayer and sang a country-Gospel song to a recording on a little boom box. I then led the community in graveside prayers in Spanish in which most of the people joined. As soon as I made the Sign of the Cross in Spanish, you could almost feel the relief among the Hispanics who must have thought, "Finally, we understand something!" One of the children from St. Catherine's Hispanic community was astonished to learn that I could speak English! She had never been at an English-speaking Mass.

After the services, several of the women went wild in their display of grief. One woman insisted that I did not sprinkle the casket correctly; I needed to make a cross on top of the casket with the water. She and others believed that if the casket does not have a cross on it, the devil could come and steal away the soul. So I made a sign of the cross with the water and my blessing. That seemed to satisfy the group.

Besides the howling and collapsing, many of them were insistent that the casket be opened one last time. This set off the husband who flew into a rage, yelling in English while the others looked on with fear and grief in their faces. Finally, with the help of another man, I led the most hysterical woman down a hill to a chair under a tree where other family members gathered. We gently led the woman to a metal chair to sit down. Unfortunately, the chair was under the blazing sun, so when her bottom touched the chair, she jumped out of the seat like a grasshopper flying out of a hot skillet with a blood-curdling scream. We finally got her calmed down.

The whole way home to Wake Forest, I kept thinking to myself, "I have got to write down this funeral experience so I don't ever forget it!"

So, I'm not going to stay up late this evening. I couldn't even if I wanted to! I'm just too wiped out. But I'm also extremely thankful for my priesthood and the most interesting life that God gave me to live!

August 5, 2002 – Monday
Wake Forest, N.C. – 6:35 p.m.
Sunny – 96 F

This has been a very wonderful day with a schedule not too filled – a day to do things at a leisurely pace.

This morning, Gael and I went to City Hall to pick up the permit to build the new rectory. The rectory address will be 246 Tyler Run Dr. We will have the rectory's phone number in the phone book, but we won't list the address in order to cut down on junk mail.

I called Bonson, the head of WKWW Architects in Charlotte, N.C. today to let him know that the five acres of land that were in dispute are officially ours to keep. Now, he and his staff can get moving on the site plan for our campuses.

In the meantime, Gael, Sue and I will be visiting some churches in the area that have balconies. We would like to get more of a feel for what balconies can be like for our own sanctuary.

I talked with a man named Angelo this morning. He is a deacon from New York where he does prison ministry. His son lives in Wake Forest, so he is thinking of moving here also. He and his wife are looking for a house. He has attended some of our Masses, and I got to meet him yesterday after the Mass in Spanish. He was wondering if there would be things to do here at St. Catherine's. I assured him that there was plenty to do. I'm looking forward to talking with him tomorrow evening after Mass.

August 7, 2002 – Wednesday
Wake Forest, N.C. – 6:40 a.m.
Sunny – 86 F

Today, I had lunch with the new minister of the United Methodist Church. She is a delightful person. Agnes, from our parish, also came to the lunch. We were the only three for the monthly Wake Forest Ministerial Association meeting.

In the afternoon, I had a very intense meeting with our school principal and the head of Catholic schools in the Diocese of Raleigh. We will be coming up with goals for the principal to accomplish. In particular, the principal will be working on increasing enrollment and retention in the school and getting the school accredited. The enrollment and retention goal will be very hard to achieve.

Before the evening Mass, I met with the new Grand Knight of our parish's Knights of Columbus Council, and we talked about some of the things the council could do this year. I'm sure that Billy will do an excellent job.

After the evening Mass, I met with Angelo, a deacon from New York. He is hoping to move down here and perhaps become a prison chaplain. I assured him that there would be things for him to do at our parish.

This morning, I received a note from the bishop showing me a hate letter he received from "E." I'll call him early this morning. I learned yesterday from the dean of my deanery that "E" once tried to destroy him also. Although I know how to deal with mentally ill persons, I am not great at working with genuine evil. "E" is a combination of mental illness and evil, perhaps in a 10 percent to 90 percent ratio. God be with me!

In Fr. Andrew M. Greeley's prayer journal, *My love: A Prayer Journal*, I read this morning something wonderful: "Help me to understand ever more clearly that I exist in an ocean of love and that no matter what happens, nothing can ever really go wrong" (p. 137).

Later – 8:00 p.m.

What an incredible day it was! I can't remember ever being so grateful for the gift of sobriety. In my drinking days, such a day would have seen me drink myself into oblivion. But in sobriety, I was able to get through this day with a sense of serenity intact.

At 8:00 a.m., Ed called me to say he resigned his position as principal of our school. Later, we talked twice, and we came up with a fine financial package to help him in his job search. He is hoping to go into business for himself. I love him and his family and wish them the very best life has to offer.

Jane, who was instrumental in founding our school, will take over as the interim administrator. She will do a super job. The head of the Catholic schools in the diocese came over in the afternoon, and we talked to the teachers to boost their morale. Mike did an excellent job.

After receiving Ed's call this morning, I went to visit the bishop. We came up with a plan to deal with "E" and her viciousness. I am delighted to say that the bishop is in my corner. He gave the go-ahead for my attorney to draft a letter to "E" advising her to get legal representation because we plan action against her behavior.

I am worn out this evening, but I am very grateful for being so severely tested all day and coming through it very well.

August 8, 2002 – Thursday – St. Dominic
Wake Forest, N.C. – 7:00 a.m.
Sunny – 84 F

On this Feast of St. Dominic, one of my favorite saints, I begin the day by asking God to be with me in a special way. And, as I do every day, I ask Mary to pray for me.

Today will be the first day without our principal, Ed. Jane will take over the ship until we can get a new principal. I will give her all the nurturing I can.

Despite all the challenges I am facing right now, I am looking forward to the day, serving the Lord as best I can.

Later – 8:45 p.m.

Well, I made it through the day in pretty good shape mentally and spiritually. Physically, I'm feeling sort of rundown, and my voice began to go away during Mass this evening. Considering all that has been going on in my life this week, I am most grateful to God for being with me in this time of stress.

The best news of the day is that the bishop is with me on my journey. I told him some new things I learned today about "E," the woman who is attacking me. It appears that since leaving St. Catherine's a year and a half ago, she has had five to six jobs. I would bet the rent that she blames her employers for not being able to keep a job. In her mind, she is never the cause of anything. I also learned that she quit her membership at another parish. When the secretary asked her which parish she was transferring to, "E" replied that she had already tried all the other Catholic parishes in the Raleigh Deanery and surrounding deaneries, and none of the parishes were able to meet her needs. She is the queen of self-righteousness!

A particularly bright spot in the day was lunch at Bennigan's with Tim. We had a nice conversation about different things I'm facing in the parish. It's good to get the perspective of a more experienced pastor. "E" tried to destroy Tim in the past also. The bishop is on to her.

Wray drafted a great letter to send to "E" telling her about an impending lawsuit. She has been advised to get legal counsel. That way, my attorney can meet with her attorney and have her stop her harmful behavior.

Today, the teachers put finishing touches on their classrooms. The Trinity Center is beautiful. I love all the bright colors and windows. It is a very pleasant place to learn. And the school folks did a remarkable job in decorating the old pre-K classroom, turning it into a beautiful "library/media center." The parish committees will love meeting there, especially the bigger ones like the Parish Council that has so many members.

August 9, 2002 – Friday
Wake Forest, N.C. – 5:25 p.m.
Sunny – 84 F

Today, our development director received formal acceptance from the International Chili Society to have a chili cook-off at our Harvest Day Festival. This is a very big deal, one of only two ICS chili cook-offs in the State of North Carolina. The publicity that we can capture from television, radio and newspapers is potentially worth a fortune. I'm very excited about this!

Last evening, I met with the incoming parents of students in kindergarten through Grade 4. The pre-K parents will be coming later, as school for pre-K 3 and pre-K 4 doesn't start for a few weeks. I think the spirit is good. With a new building and a new school leader, it's a new beginning. I talked about how critical it is to be positive in all we do. None of us can afford to be negative, as negativity drains energy. Because of the hectic lifestyles we all lead, we each need all the energy we can muster.

I put the word out to two Sister friends of mine, one an Immaculate Heart of Mary I.H.M. Sister in North Carolina and the other an Ursuline Sister in the Cleveland area, about our need for a principal. I was very surprised to receive an inquiry from a Catholic school principal in Boston. I immediately wrote him about our school and parish.

August 10, 2002 – Saturday
Wake Forest, N.C. – 7:00 p.m.
Sunny – 86 F

We're having beautiful weather—sunny and not too hot. Tomorrow, it's supposed to be around 94 F, and that's fine with me.

This evening, we had a lively 5:00 p.m. Mass. I preached about inviting God on our life journeys. Often, we begin a goal but take our sights off the goal. Then we sink, much like Peter did when he took his eyes off Jesus while walking on the water.

Following Mass, we had cookies and lemonade for the people, and then everyone was invited to tour the Trinity Center. Everyone loves its bright and cheery look.

After leaving the church, I stopped by the store to pick up some bread. As always, I used the automatic checkout in Spanish. A little girl who was standing next to her mother at the station near me asked her mother if I were Mexican! I love it!

August 11, 2002 – 19th Sunday in Ordinary Time
Wake Forest, N.C. – 8:45 p.m.
Sunny – 94 F

It was an excellent day today. My homily was relatively easy, and there was only one baptism.

The Hispanic community has decided that they would like me to explore publishing a parish bulletin completely in Spanish. I'm eager to talk with the publisher tomorrow morning.

This evening, I spent some time preparing for a luncheon meeting I'm having tomorrow with Terry Jackson of the Diocese of Raleigh. I'm preparing for him some ideas of retreats, lecture series or presentations that I could easily put together. They are:

- Adventures in American Catholic spirituality
- Developing a missionary heart
- Developing your own spirituality
- Documents of Vatican II
- Journaling and the spiritual life
- So how's your sobriety? – A life-realms approach

August 12, 2002 – Monday
Wake Forest, NC – 9:45 p.m.
Sunny day – 92 F

This evening, I went to my first Wake Forest Cultural Arts Association Board meeting. It was pretty much over my head, since the people running it didn't actually tell the newcomers (three of us) the basics of what the group does. We did have a great meal, however, and I learned about a new funky place in Wake Forest that I had never encountered before. I think I'll enjoy the group meetings—at least most of them.

August 14, 2002 – Wednesday
Wake Forest, NC – 8:45 a.m.
Sunny – 94 F

Yesterday was one of those action-packed days. It started out when I went to get my morning paper. When I checked my mailbox, I found a copy of a hate letter that "E" had sent to the bishop. He wanted me to have a copy for my files. The thrust of the letter was against another priest. I was the secondary target. It is a wonderful addition to my file on this person who is so filled with rage and hate. Rage + Hate = Evil. Nice equation.

I had a wonderful meeting with Dr. Terry Jackson at the Catholic Center. I presented him with my ideas for possible presentations that I could do. He was quite pleased with them and warned me that my phone will ring off the hook. He told me I would need to learn to say "no" to requests. We then had a delightful lunch at Rock-Ola Café on Avent Ferry Road.

Iam finding my patience is running out with the Town of Wake Forest and their delaying tactics with the parking lot permits. I am toying with the idea of beginning a fast from solid food in a few weeks if we can't get anywhere. I have to do something! With our Harvest Day Festival coming, including the international chili cook-off, we need for the lot to be finished.

The finance council met last night. We very much need to beef up our offertory giving. We are initiating a new program in September, hoping it will work. We also need to examine how much we are charging for our school. Unlike almost all other Catholic schools, for example, we have no capital fee. We cannot continue under-charging.

August 16, 2002 – Friday – St. Stephen of Hungary
Wake Forest, N.C. – 7:10 p.m.
Sunny – 92 F

On this feast of St. Stephen of Hungary, first Christian king of that nation, I think back fondly of the days I lived in Budapest while doing research. I think especially of Peter Basel and all the help he gave me, of visiting the synagogue, of going to see the hand of St. Stephen, of visiting the magnificent churches, etc. When I was there, the country was behind the Iron Curtain. Thank God those days are over and the people enjoy freedom today.

Yesterday, I went to The Corner ice cream store across from Southeastern Baptist Theological Seminary for the first time. I met Amy P. there, and we then went to her place to eat our takeout lunches. Amy is working on a degree in alternative spirituality. She lives in a delightful four-room house that is decorated to make it extremely cheerful and welcoming.

Today was a wonderful day. After Mass, a couple of parishioners came to visit. They gave me a colorful stole from Guatemala. I'll be baptizing their adopted Guatemalan child on the 31st of this month.

The rest of the day was basically my own. I spent most of the day puttering around the office getting it organized at a leisurely pace. The day also saw me welcoming new parishioners to the parish, saying goodbye to others, and visiting the school children only to find myself in an unexpected fire drill. I am so very pleased at how smoothly the school year has begun.

August 18, 2002 – 20th Sunday in Ordinary Time
Wake Forest, N.C. – 7:45 p.m.
Partly cloudy – 94 F

Today was one of my best homilies ever, judging not only by my gut instinct but also from the accolades I received from so many parishioners. I was "on fire" with the Holy Spirit.

I talked today about the concept of "universalism" in the Catholic Church. I pointed out "Catholic" means "universal," and that "universal" is the call of Jesus Christ to all humanity, in all places, in all ages to follow Him. I pointed out that there have always been people in the Church who have tried to exclude others, such as whites excluding blacks in North Carolina in the past. More common today, however, is that some people in the Church try to make others feel inferior. I pointed out that this is neither Christian nor Catholic. We must love all people equally regardless of what gifts God has given them, gifts such as their skin color, racial or ethnic background, sexual orientation, gender, eye color, country of origin and the like. All are equal. God loves all equally. All are made in the image of God.

I pointed out that not all bigots and people of hatred wear the robes of the Klan or have a swastika on their shoulders. Many are masquerading as Catholics, infecting the communities. I strongly admonished any in the congregation who might hate to hear the love message of Jesus Christ to consider joining other churches, especially those fundamentalist Protestant groups who preach a Gospel of hatred and bigotry.

This was definitely one of my most powerful homilies and one of my clearest. Thank you, Holy Spirit!

Yesterday, I went to visit the site of the new rectory. It looks so different with so many of the trees down, but I think it will be beautiful when everything is finished. There will still be plenty of trees there to make me feel cozy and in the midst of nature.

August 19, 2002 – Monday
Wake Forest, N.C. – 8:30 p.m.
Partly sunny – 96 F

This evening, I visited the RCIA program and welcomed the people. I was very happy to see a woman whom I invited last week. I also had the privilege of meeting with another woman in RCIA tonight. Though she had been baptized in a Baptist church many years ago, she has been searching all her life for a church where she felt comfortable. She reported that the moment she walked into St. Catherine's, she felt that this was "home." A friend of hers who attends St. Catherine's invited her to come to our community. Now, she is in the RCIA program.

As the day comes to a close, I know I have to prepare two homilies so I can go to the Outer Banks with my friend next Monday, but I have no energy tonight to do them. I think I know what I'm going to talk about the next two weeks: Peter and the papacy this coming week, then Oscar Romero as an example of how being a servant of God can require one to bear a heavy cross.

August 20, 2002 – Tuesday – St. Bernard
Wake Forest, N.C. – 7:00 a.m.
Partly sunny – 92 F

After saying Morning Prayers in the Breviary, one of my favorite things is to sit and read the *News & Observer* and have my favorite coffee— Café Espresso by Medaglia D'Oro. I know, I know. I shouldn't be drinking such strong stuff. I'm thinking of making coffee with half real espresso and half decaf espresso. Then I can eventually go to decaf completely.

Anyway, reading the newspaper is such an adventure. I remember a teacher I had in high school (Maryknoll Junior Seminary), who was a Maryknoll missionary priest. He told us that one of the most amazing things we could ever purchase was a daily newspaper. For just cents, we could have some of the finest writers in the nation at our fingertips. I have treasured those words and have come to fully agree.

Today, for example, I read about the various cases that the U.S. Supreme Court will tackle in their new term. The Supreme Court has always fascinated me. The issues are usually never between "right" and "wrong," but rather about two rights that collide, and the Supreme Court must decide which right must yield. I am fascinated today by a gun case that is coming up, involving a challenge to a four year Massachusetts law that forbids target practice on human images at certain gun clubs. The ban applies to clubs that have special licenses for large capacity weapons. Apparently, in this case, people are shooting at images of the current American boogeymen, Saddam Hussein and Osama bin Laden. At first blush, one might dismiss the case as irrelevant. But what if the images were of more popular persons—such as the pope, or President of the United States—or of typical targets of various hate groups such as African Americans, gay Americans, Hispanics and the like? This is all very interesting.

Two other cases that will be fascinating to watch involve challenges to a 50 year Virginia law outlawing cross burning and a federal racketeering law used against abortion clinic demonstrators.

August 21, 2002 – Wednesday – St. Pius X
Wake Forest, N.C. – 7:45 p.m.
Partly sunny – 94 F

I'm exhausted this evening, probably because I didn't get a nap today and have been running all day.

This morning, I went to my first meeting of the Bishop's Annual Appeal (BAA) Board. It was a pretty good meeting, and I got to meet many folks I haven't seen for some time.

Afterwards, I went to Duke University Medical Center for a skin check. It was a good thing I went, for they discovered a small growth on my back that they removed. They are pretty sure it is basal cell carcinoma. The young physician who saw me is a parishioner at St. Thomas More Parish in Chapel Hill, N.C. and the medical student helping him is a parishioner at Immaculate Conception in Durham, N.C., originally from Argentina.

August 23, 2002 – Friday – St. Rose of Lima
Wake Forest, N.C. – 5:40 p.m.
Sunny – 101 F

I had a wonderful discussion last evening with a couple that wish to get married in April. The man has never been baptized and plans on joining the RCIA program and becoming a Catholic. The bride's mother came to the meeting and would like to get involved in a Golden Age group. I'm thinking that now is a good time to get something going in the parish for the 55+ age group, since everything we do is for the kids and Hispanics.

Today, a former mayor of Wake Forest dropped by to visit me. He's running for the state senate, though that's not why he dropped by. He's an interesting man to talk with and we'll go out to lunch soon.

I was very happy to see in the newspaper this morning that Walmart is planning on building a Super Walmart right up the street at the corner of US 1 and US 1-A! Although I don't support Walmart's personnel policies, I like it for its low prices and vast array of merchandise. It's so much better than Target in terms of price. I know our current mayor is against Walmart, but I'm for the underdog consumer who benefits from the low prices Walmart has to offer. I know the little shop owners usually don't like Walmart because they can't begin to compete with the low prices of the giant store, but isn't that competition, and isn't competition what makes American capitalism thrive? I guess I am coming from the perspective of a consumer without much money to spend.

The house is nice and clean and ready for my guest. Now I'm working on my September 1st homily, which will be about Oscar Romero and how he suffered as a result of his preaching of the Gospel of Jesus Christ. This week, I'm talking about how God chooses men to become priests, and how His ways are not our ways. I'm using, as an example, St. Leopold Mandic, who died in 1942. He was a Franciscan Capuchin who was only 4 feet 6 inches tall, had a limp due to arthritis, and had a speech impediment so severe that he was not permitted to preach. He was also the butt of jokes from his colleagues who called him "Brother Absolve-All" because he was such a forgiving and easygoing guy. Leopold spent most of his priesthood hearing confessions—often 10-15 hours per day in a confessional that was cold in winter and hot and stuffy in the summer. The moral of the story is that like Peter when he was called, Leopold had nothing going for him in the eyes of the world. Yet, God saw into his heart, just as God saw into Peter's heart.

August 25, 2002 – 21st Sunday in Ordinary Time
Wake Forest, N.C. – 5:40 p.m.
Partly cloudy – 94 F

The weekend went very smoothly. I had only three baptisms and one presentation. One of the baptisms was Briceda Díaz and the presentation was for Armando Miguel Díaz. These are the children of Angeles and Armando Díaz, the leaders of our Latino band.

Plans for the Harvest Day Festival are going very well. Thanks to our development director, Kathleen, the festival should run much more smoothly than in recent years, take lots less work, and feature more interesting events. Among events sparking lots of interest include a pie making contest and the chili contest. I'll be in the chili contest for sure. I'm sure Fr. Charles, who will be here from Uganda for the festival, will find it very entertaining. We'll get plenty of wonderful photos from the festival that he can take back to show the people of Muduuma parish.

Now that I'm finished with next week's pastor's corner and homily, I can get into vacation mode. I look forward to my trip to the Outer Banks tomorrow.

August 27, 2002 – Tuesday
Nags Head, N.C. – 9:15 p.m.
Rain and Sun – 89 F

The trip to the Outer Banks was wild yesterday. Torrential rains dogged us for much of the trip, and Jim and I saw many cars and trucks in ditches or accidents on US 64. The newspaper today said there were many accidents due to flash floods in North Carolina. Some areas got eight inches of rain in 24 hours.

This is my first trip to the Outer Banks and Jim's first also. We're staying at the Comfort Inn on Nags Head. Yesterday, we explored Hatteras Island and had lunch at Peking Restaurant and dinner at Jockey's Ribs.

Today, we went north to the Currituck Lighthouse, passing through beautiful towns such as Kill Devil Hills, Kitty Hawk, Southern Shores, Duck, and Sanderling. I'm amazed at the incredible wealth in the real estate here on the Outer Banks. I get the impression that the towns get ritzier as one goes north; Duck and Corolla are especially nice.

Today, I walked the beach for almost three hours and got just a bit too much sun. I love being back at the ocean, though, because the ocean was my first taste of North Carolina when I came here to study for the Diocese of Raleigh in 1995.

The sights and sounds of the beach never really change. There are still the ever-busy sandpipers and mellower, more dignified gulls, the hardy sea oats and ever- changing sand dunes, parents introducing their small children to the majesty and mystery of the ocean, teenagers trying so hard to be cool and impress their friends on their surfboards, and the never-ending waves. The waves today were particularly rough, knocking me around as though I were a mere rag doll.

This evening, we went to see *My Big Fat Greek Wedding,* which we both enjoyed. It wasn't a great film, but it was funny and entertaining.

August 28, 2002 – Wednesday
Nags Head, N.C. – 6:20 p.m.
Mostly rainy – 85 F

I was able to get in an hour's walk on the beach this morning and then go into the ocean. The currents were too intense, however, and I scraped my knee when I was thrown down and dragged on the ocean floor.

We stopped at a store called Cabin Creek that is owned by a former mayor of Wake Forest. I got a 20 percent discount on my purchases because I know the owner. He had alerted the manager that I would be stopping by. I bought two beautiful decorative boats, a "Welcome" hanging, and a nautical vase. At another store, The Farmer's Daughter, I got a beautiful nautical clock. I'm trying to get sea-oriented things to decorate a room in my retirement home someday.

After lunch at the New York Pub & Pizza, Jim and I visited the Wright Brothers Museum. Most of the museum was closed, so there wasn't much to do. Jim stayed for a film on the Wright Brothers while I went shopping for some saltwater taffy. Unfortunately, I lost my new glasses at the museum, probably in the parking lot.

In one shop we learned that pirates in the area used to tie a lantern around the neck of a nag (horse) and have it go back and forth on the land. Ships would think this meant a safe harbor, and when they got close, the pirates would attack. That is how the town got its name Nags Head, at least according to this story.

August 30, 2002 – Friday
Wake Forest, N.C. – 8:00 p.m.
Rainy – 78 F

Without the rain to slow us down, it only took 3 hours and 15 minutes to get from Nags Head to Wake Forest. It used to take four hours, but with the beautiful new Dare Bridge, the time is cut considerably.

I took Jim to the airport this morning. He should get into Spokane around 7:00 p.m. Pacific time, and then he'll be home in Ronan, Mont. around 11:00 p.m. Mountain time. I think he enjoyed his stay here. I certainly enjoyed getting away.

There was the usual mountain of mail waiting for me, none of it urgent. There were a couple of very nice letters of support that I greatly appreciate. Another piece of good news is that because so many people signed up for Spanish classes at St. Catherine's, Wake Tech is offering a second class. One class will be on Saturday evenings, and the other will be on Wednesday evenings.

The rain continues to fall and is scheduled to stay around for the next several days. Though I'm delighted for the rain to help our low water supply, it is a bit depressing having gray days.

August 31, 2002 – Saturday
Wake Forest, N.C. – 9:05 p.m.
Rainy – 75 F

Adios to August! It was one heck of a month, and I'm delighted to see it go. On the other hand, it tested me like I've never been tested before in my priesthood. The test has led to a bolder, more passionate form of preaching. For that I am thankful.

This weekend, I'm preaching on the cross that all Catholic Christians are called to bear, especially church leaders. I'm talking about Oscar Romero and how he was martyred for standing up against oppression and poverty and rightwing hate groups. Though there are some priests who believe in "don't rock the boat" or "don't make waves," I believe we Catholics are called to a more radical path, preaching the dignity that all people should receive, not just the rich and powerful. Unfortunately, priests who preach a radical message often get themselves attacked or killed. But that just makes their message all the more powerful as we have seen since the early Catholics, the Apostles, who were killed for their faith. For almost 2,000 years, the Catholic Church has grown in large part because of the blood of the martyrs.

Anyway, I'm glad this month is over, and I'm anxious for a new one to begin. May God give me the strength to meet any challenges I may have, and may He protect me in the shadow of His wings.

SEPTEMBER 2002

September 1, 2002 – 22nd Sunday in Ordinary Time
Wake Forest, N.C. – 8:00 p.m.
Rainy – 65 F

As usual, I was energized by this morning's liturgies. The Hispanic community especially gives me energy. Today, Jesús talked with parents and youth, and the youth program is off to a good start. I'm eager to see the new kind of life it generates in the community. Meanwhile, we'll be having a special youth Mass each month and other exciting ministries for the Hispanic community. I am delighted to say that preaching in Spanish is becoming easier for me.

This month should be very special – one that I'm looking forward to. For example, in a couple of weeks, I'll be welcoming Fr. Charles Ntege, curate of Muduuma Parish in Uganda, and I will be going on my annual Priests' Retreat. This month, I'll also be busy getting adult education courses ready as well as a retreat for the Ladies' Guild. It will be a very busy and, I hope, productive month.

Today, I finished reading *Manic Ride*. I hope that the author, one of my parishioners, can sell it in a few weeks. If all goes well, I'll get a part in the movie. That would be an incredible adventure.

September 2, 2002 – Monday – Labor Day
Wake Forest, N.C. – 8:10 p.m.
Cloudy – 75 F

This morning, I buried a 3-month-old girl at Pine Forest Memorial Gardens. She died of SIDS and was buried in Connecticut, but now that her parents have moved down here, they brought the body down to be buried in North Carolina. Though they had grieved previously, the reburial opened up the wounds once again. My heart goes out to them.

The Latinos were busy working on my rectory today. Because of the rain last week, they didn't get much work done. In the building business, no work means no pay. I'm glad the weather held up for them today.

Tomorrow, I go for oral surgery, so I've been busy getting my Pastor's Corner done for the bulletin and getting my thoughts down on paper for this coming weekend's homily. Don is picking me up at 6:45 a.m. for my 7:45 a.m. appointment, and he'll bring me home when the surgery is done. Being knocked out is great. With IV sedation, I have absolutely no fear of the dentist!

September 3, 2002 – Tuesday, St. Gregory the Great
Wake Forest, NC – 8:00 p.m.
Partly cloudy – 88 F

The trip to Dr. Hum went well despite the heavy traffic on Capital Blvd. (US 1). He was only able to do two dental implants instead of three for some reason. I'm sure that will be okay. I have spent the rest of the day resting, taking a nap, celebrating a Mass by myself at the dining room table, and puttering around the house. I'll finish this coming weekend's homily tomorrow morning – I am always much brighter in the morning.

September 4, 2002 – Wednesday
Wake Forest, N.C. – 4:45 p.m.
Sunny – 92 F

My oral surgeon called me last evening to see how I am doing. I like that in a physician! I'm doing pretty well. My left jaw is a bit swollen and a bit stiff and sore, but I'm fine otherwise.

This has been a wonderful day off! After finishing my coming weekend's homily, I did a little shopping at the Dollar Tree and some grocery shopping. I bought some new flowers for the house.

Later, I celebrated Mass by myself and began working on my homilies for the weekends of September 15th and 22nd. I have to do them in advance because I will be going on the annual Priests' Retreat the week of September 16-20th, and Fr. Charles Ntege will be arriving on the 17th. Now that I think of it, I'd better get busy working on the homily for Sept. 29th also!

I once saw a funny diet that reflects how many people diet, but I unfortunately lost it. The other day, however, I ran across it in a book called *More Hot Illustrations For Youth Talks* (Grand Rapids, MI: Zondervan Publishing House, 1995, p. 21). It's called "A diet for losers."

BREAKFAST

½ grapefruit
1 slice whole-wheat toast
8 oz. skim milk

LUNCH

4 oz. lean broiled chicken breast
1 cup steamed zucchini
1 Oreo cookie
herb tea

MID-AFTERNOON SNACK

Rest of the package of Oreos
1 quart of rocky-road ice cream
1 jar hot fudge

DINNER

2 loaves garlic bread
Large pepperoni and mushroom pizza
Large pitcher of root beer
2 Snickers bars
Entire frozen cheesecake, eaten directly from the freezer

I wish I had written this clever diet that contains so much truth about the way things often are in the life of dieters!

September 5, 2002 – Thursday
Wake Forest, N.C. – 9:20 p.m.
Sunny – 88 F

What a great day it was today! Not only was the sun out in full force, but the humidity seemed very low.

I began the day at 6:00 a.m. as always, and I just now got home from the office. All day long, I was seeing people for one thing or another, making a hospital visit and doing troubleshooting.

The highlight of my day came this evening when I spent an hour and a half talking to a 27-year-old man named Brad. He is thinking of priesthood. I stopped Brad a couple of months ago when he was coming into Mass one Sunday, and I mentioned to him how great it was seeing him always so positive. I detected something special about him.

At the time, I also put a bug in his ear about perhaps getting involved in ministry. Last week, I asked him about whether or not he had considered doing ministry yet. He surprised me by telling me that as a matter of fact he had been thinking of something, and he had already set up an appointment to see me on Thursday evening after Mass (this evening). We'll get Brad into the Eucharistic Ministry program and the Maryknoll Affiliates, and we'll also nurture his vocation. He said that the Sunday homilies were what made him committed to coming to Mass each weekend. I love to hear things like that. God works in mysterious ways, and I'm thrilled to be part of His plan.

September 7, 2002 – Saturday
Wake Forest, N.C. – 9:20 a.m.
Sunny – 82 F

The last few days have been so hectic at the office that it was hard to take time to smell the roses, so to speak. I can see right now that I'll have to get busy preparing my presentations for the fall semester at St. Catherine's, because who knows how much time I'll have to prepare as the semester approaches.

The weather has turned absolutely beautiful! The humidity is low and the days are filled with sunshine.

The local channel, News 14 Carolina, is currently advertising the St. Raphael Fair. Perhaps we will be able to have such great coverage when we have ours on October 5th. I just hope the weather will be as beautiful.

Yesterday, I had a great meeting with a person named Janet who is from Ecuador. She is eager to do ministry in the Hispanic community. Especially, she would like to begin a Bible studies program in Spanish. She has taught Bible studies up North using the Little Rock programs that we use at St. Catherine's. What a blessing that would be! She is also willing to help with translation.

Yesterday, I received my weekly homily translation. The person translating it is new at this, so I have to have a little meeting with him. Often, Hispanics get sloppy with writing Spanish and forget to put accents. This is terrible for the non-Hispanic who needs to follow all the rules. For example, there are no such words in Spanish as *tambien* or *el dia*. On the other hand, there are these words: *también* and *el día*. These I can usually pick up, but when the translator forgets to put the accent on the vowels in unfamiliar words, it is more difficult.

September 8, 2002 – 23rd Sunday in Ordinary Time
Wake Forest, N.C. – 7:50 p.m.
Sunny – 82 F

If my parish got any more energy, I think it would explode! It is just incredible—activity everywhere in both the Anglo and Hispanic communities.

I heard this morning that the Saturday evening Spanish teacher, Juan Montas, is terrific. The students are excited. I hope the Wednesday teacher, who supposedly has pink hair, will be just as good.

I gave my homily in Spanish to one of the men in the Latino community after Mass. He is having trouble controlling his 14-year-old daughter, and my homily on fraternal correction hit the mark.

Another man, an Anglo, came up to me after Mass and said that for the last three weeks, he has felt the homilies were especially on target for his life. This is great to hear!

Toys continue to pour in for our Harvest Day Festival and the excitement builds. This year, we're having a dance the evening before the festival. The St. Catherine Latino Band will play at the 5:00 p.m. Mass on October 5th, while *Soul Purpose*, our Praise & Worship Band, will play for the festival. I pray the weather will be cooperative!

Tomorrow, I will begin looking for some help for an 11-year-old girl who is pregnant for the second time. The girl's mother would like her daughter to carry the baby till near term, then have a C-section and have the baby adopted by a fine Hispanic family. The first baby was aborted. This experience will help me learn what kind of help is available in the community.

This week, I'm going to try my hardest to find out about our parking lot and how we can get a permit. Enough time has passed and my patience has just about run out.

September 9, 2002 – Monday
Wake Forest, N.C. – 5:25 p.m.
Sunny – 84 F

Today, Bob Neal swung by the office, and we picked out the color of siding for the house. It'll be a medium green with sort of a beige trim. I think it will blend into the woods pretty well.

A reporter for *The Wake Weekly* also stopped by to take my photo for a special feature they are doing on reflections of September 11th, 2001. It's hard to believe a whole year has passed already!

Rosa and I spent about an hour this morning discussing the contents of the new Spanish bulletin. I am amazed at all the different people we now have heading up various ministries in the Hispanic community! What phenomenal growth.

Then this afternoon, Kathleen sent me a copy of the Migrant Ministry grant she has put together. We are applying for funds for a bus and literature in Spanish that we can take to the migrant worker camps.

September 10, 2002 – Tuesday
Wake Forest, N.C. – 10:00 p.m.
Mostly sunny – 84 F

Last evening, I went to my second meeting of the Wake Forest Cultural Arts Association Board. It was a much more comfortable experience than the first meeting. I invited the group to have a free table at the St. Catherine of Siena Harvest Day Festival on October 5th.

Today, I had my first visit with my new spiritual director, Fr. Dan. We had a great chat. I'm sure this will develop into a great relationship. Dan has the qualities I look for in a spiritual director: down-to-earth, a good sense of humor and levelheaded. Among other things, we talked about what a great thing it is to be priests in our respective parishes and this diocese. Our parishes are exploding in size, and the Diocese of Raleigh has doubled since 1990. What an adventure!

I was able to send some of the material for the cover of our new Spanish parish bulletin to Cleveland, Ohio this afternoon. The first edition is to appear on Sunday, October 13th.

Today is primary election day in North Carolina. I voted at the Wake Forest Community House, and when I came out of the building, I ran into Dr. Tom Jackson, Pastor of Wake Forest Baptist Church. Tom and I are good friends, and he wanted to introduce me to just about everyone who came along. It is great to be in a community like Wake Forest where people are so friendly.

We had a Mass this evening in memory of those who lost their lives on September 11th, 2001. I talked about how fortunate we are to be in our parish and country, and I talked about the fragility of human life. I also noted how I appreciate the little things of life so much more – things such as lit candles glowing in my living room, fresh flowers on the coffee table, a comfortable green chair, television and solitude. It doesn't take much to make me happy!

September 11, 2002 – Wednesday
Wake Forest, N.C. – 8:10 a.m.
Sunny – 88 F

Today is the first anniversary of the tragedy of September 11th, 2001, and there is peace in our land. Tropical Storm Gustav has left the Outer Banks where it left lots of rain moving up to the Cape Cod area. North Carolina still has two Miss America candidates. And in the primaries yesterday, Erskine Bowles (D) will square off against Elizabeth "Liddy" Dole (R) for U.S. Senate in the November elections. This evening, I will go to Our Lady of Lourdes to concelebrate a special Mass commemorating September 11th.

This morning, there was a beautiful article called "Getting to the Heart of America" by R.J. Del Vecchio the *News & Observer* (Wed., Sept. 11, 2002, p. 15A). It is about an Indian Hindu man who talks about what a great privilege it is to become an American. As a writer, such inspirational articles cause me to reflect on the nature of writing. The blank page is filled with unlimited possibilities. I can choose to write something negative or trivial, or I can write something inspirational and uplifting. The choice is 100 percent mine. May the Holy Spirit help remind me of this choice in all my writing endeavors.

September 12, 2002 – Thursday
Wake Forest, N.C. – 9:40 p.m.
Sunny – 82 F

I'm totally exhausted today as I write this, having been going non-stop since 6:00 a.m. when I left the house for Duke University. I just got home from a deanery meeting around 9:00 p.m.

Today, I had my annual IV-med Stress Test at Duke University Medical Center in the morning, and this afternoon, I saw my cardiologist, Dr. Robert Califf. It seems that last year when my test was read, there was about 10 percent that was fuzzy. The physician was not concerned about that. This year, however, 30 percent of my heart is ischemic, or not receiving enough oxygen. I'll be scheduling a cardiac catheterization probably after Fr. Charles leaves for Uganda. At that time, we'll see if I need another angioplasty or heart surgery.

This evening, we had a Raleigh Deanery meeting at St. Raphael's. The various parishes talked about the highlights of what is going on in their parishes. The bishop attended this meeting and he was especially impressed with the fact that 42 percent of St. Catherine's is composed of youth 19 years old and younger. He is also impressed that we're having a chili cook-off.

The bishop also talked with me about the person who attacked me via a right-wing attorney. Yesterday, the bishop sent me a copy of a letter from the Apostolic Nunciature of the United States of America. It talked about how that office had received a letter from the attacker's attorney and that the Apostolic Nuncio's office would not "insert itself" into this case. Rather, because the bishop of Raleigh is more familiar with the attack, it would be up to him to "resolve this matter in a manner you [the bishop] deem suitable." Great news indeed!

This evening, I talked with a fellow priest about co-authoring a journal article with Wray Harrison and myself, and he agreed to this endeavor. I'll put together the rationale along with a preliminary outline. The article will focus on priests who have been libeled or slandered by private citizens and what should be the stance of civil law, Canon law and the priests in question. I believe it is a very timely topic that would make good reading and serve as a springboard for some very important discussion.

September 15, 2002 – 24th Sunday in Ordinary Time
Wake Forest, N.C. – 8:15 p.m.
Rainy and Cloudy – 78 F

Two people in the parish have died this weekend, so we'll have a funeral on Tuesday morning and perhaps one on Wednesday. Both of the men who died received the Sacrament of the Sick and had suffered for a long while.

I scheduled my cardiac catheterization for Tuesday, October 22nd. Fr. Charles will return to Uganda on October 19th and I will be able to preach that weekend in Pinehurst, N.C. for World Mission Sunday.

On Monday the 21st, I'll be able to do my Documents of Vatican II course. So, October 22nd looks like a fine day for me to have the procedure done. I'll carry an overnight bag in case I have an angioplasty, or whatever.

This weekend was Catechetical Weekend, so we had a special blessing for all our St. Catherine's catechists. We have approximately 100 of them. Thank God for all the wonderful work they do – we have about 900 kids studying the Faith at St. Catherine's.

September 16, 2002 – Monday – SS Cornelius & Cyprian
Wake Forest, N.C. – 10:00 a.m.
Rainy – 84 F

Tropical Storm Hanna is bringing much needed rain to the Triangle. The reporters don't think it's enough, but every little bit helps in this drought. The little stream in back of my house, usually invisible, was gushing with water earlier this morning.

It's just 10:00 a.m., and already I have been to the church to deliver some clean linen, give directions to the secretaries about tomorrow's funeral and other items, finish this coming Sunday's Spanish homily on registration, and write my weekly Pastor's Corner. Now, I can do some grocery shopping and desk cleaning in my study and celebrate a private Mass at my kitchen table. Around 5:00 p.m., I'll head down to Wrightsville Beach, N.C. to hear the opening remarks of our bishop at the annual Diocese of Raleigh Priests' Retreat.

September 17, 2002 – Tuesday – St. Robert Bellarmine
Wake Forest, N.C. – 9:25 p.m.
Sunny – 84 F

Today featured a funeral, two dental appointments, mowing the lawn and picking up Fr. Charles Ntege at the airport. Charles is delighted to be in our country from Uganda. I'm looking forward to his visit.

September 18, 2002 – Wednesday
Wrightsville Beach, N.C. – 8:50 p.m.
Partly Cloudy – 86 F

It was a great, but exhausting, day. Fr. Charles survived his first full day in America and is fascinated by all the "stuff" that surrounds us in this country.

The trip to Wrightsville Beach was fine. Before getting to the island, we stopped at St. Mark's where I spent my first two years of priesthood. Naturally, I had to say hello and give hugs to the whole staff. They still remember me fondly. The new school building is beautiful, and the sanctuary is more elegant in its simplicity than I remembered.

The visiting funeral priest said the funeral he did at St. Catherine's went well, but there was a power outage during part of it. He said that just when he was making an important point, the power went back on.

I have asked God for some healing on this retreat—healing that shows itself in a sense of serenity. I also ask for an increase in trust of God that He will always protect me from harm.

September 19, 2002 – Thursday, St. Januarius
Wrightsville Beach, N.C. – 8:25 p.m.
Sunny – 86 F

Today was quite wonderful. I'm especially glad that I am getting to know more and more of the priests more intimately. This makes for more of a sense of priestly fraternity. Many of the priests whom I don't know very well seem to know me from my mission work, frequent exposure in *NC Catholic*, and from my experiences at St. Catherine's.

Everyone has been very welcoming to Fr. Charles. Msgr. Jerry Lewis said he was talking to Fr. Bill, head of the diocesan Society for the Propagation of the Faith, and congratulated him on the fine job he is doing for the missions. Jerry told him, though, that he might have created a monster missionary-type—Bob Kus. What a great compliment!

Today, I spent about an hour and a half in the ocean. The day was filled with sunshine, the ocean did not have riptides and the water was warm.

The sky was crystal clear blue with some of the fluffy white clouds that I like so much.

Fr. Mac, with whom I was ordained, joined me for a bit. We reminisced about our seminarian days and talked of the crazy things that we have experienced as priests. One thing that struck me as being so bizarre in my first year of priesthood was a diocesan priest study retreat held at a fancy golf resort where rooms were $150 per night and the meals were fit for a king. Our retreat topic that time was about how to become more sensitive to the needs of the poor.

I had a very enjoyable time with my friend Arturo also. He's probably my best friend in the priesthood, though I have several others with whom I'm close. His parish is thinking of adopting a sister parish in his native Colombia. Perhaps Arturo and I will go to Colombia together some day.

At our normal retreat banquet, we had a very interesting table. Besides the three Americans, we had priests from Congo, Uganda, Colombia, Vietnam and a Missionhurst Brother from Indonesia. We nicknamed our table the "U.N. Table."

September 20, 2002 – Friday – Korean Martyrs
Wake Forest, N.C. – 5:00 p.m.
Sunny – 86 F

The closing Mass of the retreat was very moving. Several of us, including Fr. Charles and myself, received the Sacrament of the Sick. When someone asked me if I was receiving it mostly for a physical problem, I answered, "Well, mostly for my spirit. And mind. And body." We cracked up laughing. I could use all the Spirit's help in every area of life!

September 21, 2002 – Saturday
Wake Forest, N.C. – 6:45 p.m.
Partly cloudy – 81 F

Today, we began our parish's Fall Stewardship weekend. In the Anglo community, we're focusing on increasing our offertory, which has been too low, while in the Hispanic community, we will be focusing on registration into the parish. I pray that we will be successful in this stewardship campaign!

Today, I signed nine letters of welcome to new households who have joined the parish this week. This brings us to 37 new households in the past three weeks!

September 22, 2002 – 25th Sunday in Ordinary Time
Wake Forest, N.C. – 6:20 p.m.
Sunny – 86 F

Fr. Charles survived one of my typical Sundays and its four Masses. He described the parish as "hectic," but very friendly. In addition to the usual chaos caused by all the kids of the parish coming and going, we had the Cub Scouts selling popcorn; the Harvest Day Festival folks selling tickets for rides, the dance and raffle tickets; the Knights of Columbus signing up volunteers for their annual Tootsie Roll campaign; and our finance director and development director helping people with the Electronic Funds Transfer forms.

Since yesterday, Fr. Charles has been invited to attend a football game, a soccer game, tour the capital in Raleigh, and go to Washington, D.C. with the Anglo youth group! I think his stay here will be quite memorable for him.

I believe the talk with the Anglo community about the need to increase our offertory went well. Now, we'll see if the offertory goes up in the coming weeks.

The Hispanic community came through with flying colors in the registration drive. The registration process went very smoothly, and we had plenty of volunteers to help people with filling out their forms. Today's parable was from Matthew's Gospel (20:1-16), about the workers who were hired at different hours of the day to work in the vineyard. At the end of the day, all were treated equally – that is, all were given a full day's wage. I likened this parable to the Catholic Church in America. At first, only Catholics from England, Spain and France were here. Then came those from Italy, Bohemia, Germany, Ireland and Africa. Later came people from the Philippines, Korea and Vietnam. And now it is the Hispanics from the New World's turn. And though they are the newcomers to the American Church, they are fully equal to those who have been here for many years. They have full privileges. They also have full responsibilities, and one of those responsibilities is to register in a parish of their choice. After the Mass, we had doughnuts, orange juice and coffee for the Hispanic community.

Jesús talked to me about his experience in the diocese at a Youth Certificate Program he attended. He said that St. Catherine's seems to be way ahead of just about all the other parishes in terms of Hispanic ministry. I was delighted to hear that! I know we are extremely blessed with great leadership in our Hispanic community, and I have empowered the people.

During the night, I tossed and turned. In the morning, I felt that perhaps the Holy Spirit had been wrestling with me. I woke up with what I think is a brilliant plan! I have an idea on how to make this parish a Full Stewardship parish. I have to run the idea by the parish's finance council and diocesan stewardship officials first, but I think I know of a way that St. Catherine's can be like the parish in Wichita, Kan. that does Full Stewardship. If I can pull this off—or rather if WE can pull this off—we would be able to build a church and all the other buildings without ever having to have a capital campaign! What a concept!

September 23, 2002 – Monday
Wake Forest, N.C. – 5:25 p.m.
Partly Cloudy – 71 F

What an interesting day this has been! First, I learned that we registered 101 new Hispanic households yesterday. That's a great start. We will keep registering people when they come for Baptism preparation classes and at other occasions.

After Mass, I went to visit two people at their homes. The first was a 94-year-old woman who has decided that, after a lifetime of being Catholic, she no longer wishes to be Catholic. Her anti-Catholic daughter was with her during my visit, and it took all the graces of God to help me to be completely kind to the daughter. I let the older woman know that in the Catholic Church, we believe that each person must follow his or her conscience, be it in truth or in error. I told her that I will think of her fondly and continue to pray for her and asked her to pray for me. I left on the best of terms with both women.

The next visit was to a woman in her 80s who has multiple health problems. She shared her life situation with me, and we had a very pleasant visit. Her mentally-challenged son was outdoors mowing the lawn when I arrived. To keep herself busy, she sews clothes for the preemies at WakeMed. This is part of the Threads of Love ministry of St. Catherine's Ladies' Guild. She also told me how much she enjoys coming to the soup suppers that we have during Lent. I'm glad she told me that, because it is often these little things that "make church" for elderly people. I celebrated the Sacrament of the Sick with her.

I then went to visit with Wray about our parish council tomorrow night, and then we went out to lunch at Applebee's on Six Forks Road with John, the author of the screenplay, *Manic Ride.* We are hoping that within the next couple of weeks, the movie contracts will be signed. I am to play the role of a psychiatric nurse in the film. What an adventure!

This evening, we'll be having the first meeting of the Principal Search Committee. Our task is to list the criteria for choosing the new principal of our school.

September 26, 2002 – Thursday
Wake Forest, N.C. – 4:15 p.m.
Cloudy with slight showers – 74 F

The rectory is coming along very well. Both Gael and Fr. Charles have gone to see it with me. The roof is nearly on, so the workers will be able to work even in the rain. Being snuggled in the woods gives it a warm ambience.

The Principal Search Committee has determined the characteristics we would like to see in a principal. The most important things we are looking for are maturity and wisdom, and many other leadership qualities we are putting under the broad heading of "personality." The candidates should also be computer savvy, possess financial and budgeting skills, be a practicing Catholic (diocesan policy), and have the correct professional credentials.

I brought the idea of becoming a Full Stewardship parish up with the Parish Council the other night, and they were fascinated with the idea. I'm sure that we are going to have a lot of discussion about this concept.

Fr. Charles and I went to Duke University yesterday. I had to have a small skin cancer on my back removed. Today, I took Fr. Charles to the Catholic Center for a meeting of the Bishop's Annual Appeal Committee. He was able to compare how we do things with how things are done in the Kampala Archdiocese.

September 27, 2002 – Friday – St. Vincent de Paul
Wake Forest, N.C. – 4:25 p.m.
Partly cloudy – 88 F

This morning, Fr. Charles and I went to St. Raphael's to visit with Fr. Shay. I got some great ideas for our Hispanic ministry, and I got a copy of the *Misal* from Mexico that we are planning on using in our bulletin.

After talking with Fr. Shay, we stopped to say hello to the new pastor, Fr. Fran. It turns out that he is also a Ph.D. sociologist! Now I have a colleague in the priesthood with whom to compare notes.

We stopped at Borders bookstore on our way home and got Fr. Charles a copy of *The HarperCollins Encyclopedia of Catholicism* edited by Richard P. McBrien. That is such an incredible treasure trove of information. I know Fr. Charles will treasure it for all his life. Now, I'm ordering him some books of stories for preaching such as the series by Brian Cavanaugh. The resources in Uganda are very limited, so anything we can offer from the United States is greatly appreciated.

Our Maryknoll Affiliate meeting went very well last evening, and Fr. Charles talked to the people about life in his parish and some of the exciting things our missionaries will encounter. It seems that the Sunday after arriving in Uganda, our missionaries will go to the cathedral in Kampala to celebrate the special day devoted to celebrating the Archdiocese of Kampala. One of our new missionaries is lending our other missionaries his video camera to take along.

We are also planning on sending 10 people for an immersion experience in San Pedro Sula, Honduras in March during spring break. There will be six teens and four adults. I'm guessing that they will help build houses for the poor with the parishioners.

September 29, 2002 – 26ᵗʰ Sunday in Ordinary Time
Wake Forest, N.C. – 6:30 p.m.
Sunny – 78 F

It's been a beautiful weekend with sunny skies and fair weather. Fr. Charles went to a North Carolina State University football game yesterday with a couple of our parishioners and had a terrific time. Fortunately, NC State beat U Mass by 56-24. Today, Fr. Charles went to see one of our parishioners play soccer in his league.

This evening, I showed Fr. Charles the awesomeness of the Internet. We talked about how an investment in a computer and Internet opens the entire world to one's fingertips. Teachers in his parish could use the Internet to look up virtually anything, print it out and have it for teaching. Because the education of the youth is the priority of both priests of Muduuma Parish, I can't think of anything that would be a better investment.

September 30, 2002 – Monday – St. Jerome
Wake Forest, N.C. – 8:00 p.m.
Sunny – 84 F

Well, another month comes to a close. I thank God for the graces received this month, and I look forward to a wonderful October, one of my favorite months.

I learned today that we won't be able to get the lower parking lot finished in time for our annual Harvest Day Festival on Saturday, but that's life.

OCTOBER 2002

October 2, 2002 – Wednesday – Guardian Angels
Wake Forest, N.C. – 8:07 a.m.
Sunny – 87 F

October has come in beautifully—sunny days without much humidity and cool nights for sleeping. According to The Weather Channel, Saturday should be a sunny day for our Harvest Day Festival.

Last evening, I had a visit from a young couple in their early 30s. I thought that they were visiting to begin their wedding plans, but it turned out that they came to see me as a third party to help them discern if marriage was for them. The young woman very much wanted to get married, but the man admitted that in his heart he did not want to get married. He had been afraid to tell his fiancée about this for fear of hurting her. Wisely, he knew in his heart that if he would go ahead with a wedding simply to avoid hurting her, he would eventually develop resentments through the years. It was a sad experience, yet it was good. Perhaps this interaction helped prevent a divorce and much unhappiness in the future. Now, the woman can move on, and so can the man. I will pray for them.

Yesterday, I had two dental appointments on different sides of town, and today I am running around hither and thither and yon—barbershop, camera shop, grocery store to get stocked up for the Great Chili Challenge on Saturday, dentist and office supply store. Plus, I'll mow the lawn and work on my Documents of Vatican II course. It should be a wonderful day filled with many interesting things.

Fr. Charles is out this morning with our parish custodian and his wife. They're going to breakfast, then to two museums in Raleigh before having lunch.

Later – 5:45 p.m.

I have just finished a handout for the Documents of Vatican II class that begins on October 7th. It tells the students the general format for each of the six presentations, gives an historical background of the Council and the document under discussion *Sacrosanctum Concilium* (Constitution on the Sacred Liturgy), and highlights the major points—or the "so what's the big deal"—of the document. I'm pleased with the format.

October 3, 2002 – Thursday
Wake Forest, N.C. – 3:00 p.m.
Sunny – 87 F

The weather continues to be beautiful. In fact, we are setting, or nearly setting, highs for this time of year. The only clues that fall is here are the earlier sunsets, a few leaves turning red and gold and cooler evenings. Otherwise, it is like summertime.

This morning was crazy at the office, one thing after another. Our staff is going to have a little retreat time together later in the month. We'll be looking at our accomplishments of this past year, goals that have not been accomplished, and new goals we would like to accomplish. We will also be talking about ways we can make working at St. Catherine's even better for ourselves. Kathleen has asked each of us to bring in a slogan or saying that is personally meaningful.

The first of the Harvest Day Festival trucks arrived at 7:55 a.m., a Coca-Cola truck. Fortunately, I was present to direct it where to park.

I took Fr. Charles on a walk in the woods this afternoon after our staff meeting to get a feel of our land. The possibilities for a beautiful St. Catherine campus are endless! We are so very blessed in the land department!

October 4, 2002 – Friday – St. Francis of Assisi
Wake Forest, N.C. – 7:00 p.m.
Partly cloudy – 84 F

As I write this, the house smells of two huge batches of chili that I'm making for the Great Chili Challenge that we're having tomorrow at the St. Catherine Harvest Day Festival. I had to buy a larger crockpot to hold all the chili I'm making. The chili for the blind-taste judging may not have beans or pasta, while the chili that is judged by popular vote must have beans or pasta. I'll just take a little bit of chili out for the judges before adding the dark red kidney beans.

Last evening, Fr. Charles, our two Maryknoll Affiliates who are going to Uganda (Jeff Garrett and Anne Perrotta), and I went to a meeting of the "Uganda Pilgrims" in Cary, N.C. The meeting was called by St. Michael The Archangel parishioners and friends who went to Uganda this summer. They were exploring ways that they could continue to help the people of Uganda. After much discussion, they decided to focus on just one project, supporting a school that needs help. The school is in the parish run by Fr. Emmanuel Katongole's brother, who is pastor there. I forget the name of the diocese this parish is in, but it's not in the Kampala Archdiocese where our sister parish is. Besides the St. Michael's folks were Msgr. Tom Hadden, Diocesan Vicar for African American Ministry, and Msgr. Mike Shugrue, Vicar General of the Diocese who went to Uganda with this group.

The parish is in high gear today. All of the school children celebrated Mass this morning as they do on every First Friday. They prayed for the children of Uganda and for Fr. Charles and his stay at our parish.

The *News & Observer* featured the Diocese of Raleigh this morning. Specifically, it noted that while many dioceses in the United States are hurting financially due to the scandals that have rocked the Church, our diocese is doing great. Our diocese's first capital campaign, called *God's Work—Our Challenge*, has officially ended. The goal of the campaign was $30 million. We raised $57,061,257 or 190 percent of the goal! Of this amount, 56 percent goes to the Diocese of Raleigh, and 44 percent goes to the parishes. Needless to say, we are all very pleased. This evening, WRAL-TV did a special on the success of the campaign. Of all the parishes in the diocese, the special featured St. Catherine's new Trinity Center made possible by *God's Work—Our Challenge* funds.

This evening, I stopped by the church and the dining room is decorated beautifully with little white Christmas lights, strobe lights, tables covered with linen and glowing fall candles, fall flowers and leaves, etc. The dance begins at 7:00 p.m. and ends at 11:00 p.m.

I also dropped by the rectory. It's getting bigger and bigger and looks terrific. I'm really going to enjoy living there! The covered porch off the kitchen is now being built and many of the windows are now in place.

October 5, 2002 – Saturday
Wake Forest, N.C. – 7:00 p.m.
Sunny

What an incredibly busy day this has been, yet what a wonderful one it was! We were all very grateful that we didn't have rain for our annual Harvest Day Festival. The temperature neared 90 degrees. The sun beat down on those of us that were at the Great Chili Challenge. There were lots of sunburns today. Fr. Charles and I were at the campus at 8:30 this morning for Blessing of the Animals that took place at 9:00 a.m., and we got home around 6:45 p.m. I think we'll both sleep very well tonight!

I was able to get some good photos for *The Wake Weekly*. Especially good was a photo of twin girls in a carriage who each had a frilly hat and sunglasses, and one with a dad and his two sons sitting on the sidewalk.

I tied for 4th place in the Great Chili Challenge. Someone who tasted all the chili told me that I would have won if my chili had more "kick" to it. Perhaps next year, I'll spice it up some.

The Mass this evening was interesting. We had Mass in English, music in Spanish, a baptism in English, and a Presentation in the Temple in Spanish—something for everybody!

October 6, 2002 – 27th Sunday of Ordinary Time
Wake Forest, N.C. – 5:10 p.m.
Sunny – 77 F

Technology is so great when a person knows how to use it! I looked at the photos I took at the Harvest Day Festival. They turned out great. Unfortunately, I can't seem to figure out how to get them into my Paint Shop Pro 7 folder. I'm sure it's something very simple, but right now, it's over my head. Oh, well. I'll try putting the photos on a CD and then see if I can work with them that way.

This evening, I'm going to write my second Mensaje del Padre Bob column for our new all-Spanish bulletin. The purpose of this column is twofold. Sometimes, it will be a vehicle for giving my thoughts on various topics, or to keep the Hispanic community updated on parish events.

Other times, I will use the column to teach the folks about the Church. I'll use the next column to talk about the purpose of the column and some of the things the community can expect from it. I'm looking forward to this new vehicle. Some of my writings will come from those I did for The Lion's Roar, journal of St. Mark's Parish in Wilmington.

Today, a woman stopped me at church to let me know how much she is enjoying the Spanish class she's taking. She's in our Wednesday class. Apparently, the students are designing a mystery story using their new vocabulary. In the story, there is a murder, and I'm one of the suspects, as is some of the other staff. The students are obviously having a great time!

October 7, 2002 – Monday – Our Lady of the Rosary
Wake Forest, N.C. – 10:15 p.m.
Partly sunny – 84 F

Today was one of those days that flew by so fast that I did very few of the tasks I wanted to get done. Besides a visit to WakeMed to see a parishioner recovering from knee surgery and a visit to the dentist, I took Fr. Charles to see St. Francis of Assisi parish in Raleigh. That is one of my favorite parishes. I also sent some photos of our Harvest Day Festival to *The Wake Weekly*.

This evening, I held the first of the Documents of Vatican II series. We covered the document *Sacrosanctum Concilium* (The Constitution on the Sacred Liturgy). We had 15 people in the group, and I believe it went very well. There was plenty of good discussion, and people didn't hesitate to share. I showed them a couple of minutes of a Mass I concelebrated in Cherekula, Uganda to show that although the externals of the Mass may be different in other cultures, the essence is the same.

October 10, 2002 – Thursday
Wake Forest, N.C. – 9:35 p.m.
Rainy – 74 F

As I write this, a gentle rain is falling on our town. Fortunately, I mowed the lawn yesterday.

Early this morning, I went through the new rectory with Bob Neal. We picked the places that the electric switches will go. I have to go back this weekend to figure out where to put the phone jacks and cable TV lines. The house is going to be magnificent!

I also conducted a funeral this morning at Bright's Funeral Home. The man was Catholic but never joined our parish. His wife said that in the years they were married, he only went to church about 10 times. He was only 53 years old. Apparently, he had some very serious illnesses, but only he and his physician knew their extent. The man did not share this information with his family and friends, so his death was quite a shock.

On Tuesday evening, the finance council approved planning for our parish to become a Full Stewardship parish. It is going to take a tremendous amount of work, but it will be worth it if it works! I have put together a dynamite committee that I hope will meet within the next two weeks.

October 13, 2002 – 28th Sunday in Ordinary Time
Wake Forest, N.C. – 5:40 p.m.
Cloudy – 74 F

The hot weather has gone for now, and the next few days are supposed to be even cooler, with the highs only in the upper 60s F. The recent rain has helped reduce the drought somewhat, but the drought has caused a lot of devastation in many areas, especially among the poor.

Things move quickly in my life as always. Yesterday, Dave Mayer came with me to visit the new rectory. Bob Neal, the contractor, was there with some other workers. They were putting up the deck beside the screened-in porch. Dave and I decided where to put the TV cables, computer high-speed cable, and phone jacks. I'm already planning on planting lots of new pine trees around the porch and deck.

On Friday morning, two men from the Boy Scouts of America came to visit me. The one was a young man who lives right by the church and is a member of our parish. He was hoping to be the Scoutmaster of a new Boy Scout troop at our parish. It seems that many of our Cub Scouts are getting ready to be in the Boy Scouts, and they would prefer to stay at St. Catherine's. The other man was a paid official of the Boy Scouts in the Triangle area. I told them that they would be most welcome to have a troop here at St. Catherine's, but that they would have to be in harmony with Catholic teaching. Specifically, I told them they would have to sign a document saying that they would not discriminate against people on the basis of sexual orientation. The Catholic parishioner readily agreed, but the official became very hostile and refused to sign such a document. Continuing bigotry was a more important value to him and his organization than the love of others that Jesus Christ taught.

This weekend, we had many exciting things happening at St. Catherine's. At the 9:00 a.m. Mass, we had the Rite of Welcome for the new members of the RCIA class. There were about 20 people there plus their sponsors. At the other four Masses, we had a formal Blessing of Missionaries for Jeff Garrett and Anne Perrotta. I blessed these Maryknoll Affiliates of our parish and gave them missionary crucifixes. The people very much enjoyed being part of their upcoming adventure.

Finally, our new all-Spanish bulletin appeared today and it was a hit. I imagine that it won't be long before we have to add a new page. The cover remains basically the same from week to week, and page four is advertisements. That leaves just two pages to cover all we want to cover. The graphics were absolutely super, making the whole thing very pleasant to the eye.

This weekend, John D. is on the road to finalize the selling of his movie. St. Catherine's will get 10 percent of the initial sale. I pray that all goes well.

Meanwhile, hate and violence cover the globe. There was a murder-suicide at NC State University over the weekend. The sniper who has been killing people in Maryland is still at large. And at least 183 people were killed in a bombing in Bali today. Government sources believe it was the work of Al Qaeda.

This evening, I'm putting the finishing touches on my presentation for tomorrow evening on *Lumen Gentium* (Dogmatic Constitution on the Church).

October 16, 2002 – Wednesday
Wake Forest, N.C. – 9:10 p.m.
Rainy to cloudy – 61 F

Yesterday, the staff of St. Catherine's had a mini-reflection day in the backroom of La Foresta restaurant, followed by lunch. The main thing we did was to take stock of our accomplishments for the 2001-2002 fiscal year and begin listing our accomplishments of the 2002-2003 fiscal year. It's amazing how many things we have done! No wonder I'm tired!

I received some very good news yesterday as well. I learned that I have overpaid taxes for both the federal and state governments for this year, so I don't owe any more money! And I thought I would owe at least $2,250 more. I also learned that I should be in the new rectory by Thanksgiving instead of Christmas. That would be terrific! I'd better begin packing at least some of the books.

Debbie from the diocese invited our parish's director of religious education and me to speak at a Center for Applied Research in the Apostolate (CARA) Conference on Diversity in Ministry that the diocese is hosting on November 5th and 6th. The focus of the conference is on Hispanic ministry. Specifically, we're supposed to talk about the challenges of Hispanic ministry at our parish and how we are meeting these challenges. Sue, the director of religious education, will speak at the November 5th conference for the laity, and I'll be speaking to the priests. I'm happy that we have some new things to pass out: our Hispanic registration form and our new Spanish bulletin. We were chosen because of our parish's rapid increase in Hispanic population.

Today, Fr. Charles and I went to the meeting of the Bishop's Annual Appeal (BAA) Steering Committee. It seems that another parish has gone to Full Stewardship and was able to build a new sanctuary without needing a capital campaign. Needless to say, we'll be exploring this.

October 19, 2002 – Saturday
Pinehurst, N.C. – 8:05 p.m.
Sunny – 70F

I write this note from Sacred Heart rectory in the "Golf Capital of the World." This is the very house I lived in when I first came to the Diocese of Raleigh from Cleveland to do my seminarian pastoral year—1995-1996. I am here to celebrate World Mission Sunday at this parish thanks to an invitation I received from the pastor, Fr. Bill Pitts, who is also head of the Society for the Propagation of the Faith in our diocese.

After helping with Reconciliation, I preached at the 4:30 p.m. Mass about St. Catherine's sister parishes in San Pedro Sula, Honduras and Muduuma, Uganda. I was very warmly received, and I was amazed at how many people remembered me from my days here as a seminarian and came up after Mass to say hello. Several of them told me of their own visits to Central America and Africa.

As I write this, Fr. Charles and our St. Catherine Maryknoll Affiliates are in the air flying to New York City on the first leg of their journey to Uganda. I'm going to be thinking of them and sending prayers their way every day.

On the way to Pinehurst, I saw a Christian store on US 1 called "The Carpenter's Shop." After browsing around the store, I bought a book called *Bryson City Tales* that takes place in Bryson City, N.C. It contains stories of a physician's first year in the Great Smokey Mountains. I visited Bryson City as a seminarian while touring Southern Appalachia to learn about the problems of the people. I think this will be a very interesting book and give me insights into my own autobiographical writings as a priest, psychiatric nurse and sociologist.

October 20, 2002 – 29th Sunday in Ordinary Time: World Mission Sunday
Wake Forest, N.C. – 7:10 p.m.
Cloudy – 72 F

It was a great pleasure visiting Pinehurst this weekend. Today, I met so many people from the past. I learned that some of the ministries I started as a seminarian—Bible Studies, hospital ministry, adult servers and girl servers—are still thriving.

It's good to get out of town even if it is only for 24 hours.

October 22, 2002 – Tuesday
Wake Forest, N.C. – 6:15 a.m.
Rainy – 64 F

The presentation on the Vatican II document, *Unitatis Redintegratio* (Decree on Ecumenism), went very well. I'm learning a great deal by offering this series, and I think the participants are enjoying it also.

My little overnight bag is packed, and I'm writing this while waiting for Sue Gammon to pick me up to take me to Duke University Medical Center where I'll have a cardiac catheterization this morning. I suspect I'll have to stay overnight, as I think they'll probably have to do an angioplasty. I'm sure all will go well. At least I'll have two full days off!

October 23, 2002 – Wednesday
Durham, N.C. – Duke University Medical Center – 9:00 a.m.
Sunny – 70 F

I write this from Duke University Medical Center. It's a beautiful sunny morning, I just finished breakfast, and I'm sitting up for the first time in 24 hours.

Yesterday, Sue and I arrived at Duke promptly at 7:30 a.m. I didn't go for a cardiac catheterization until around noon, and then I had to wait until around 4:00 p.m. before going for an angioplasty and stent implant. The circumflex artery was nearly completely blocked. All went well, and the blood is flowing well to my heart again. One of the physicians came to bring me a "before and after" shot of the heart—quite a dramatic difference!

During the night, the R.N. gave me extra fluids because my blood pressure was staying at 80/50. This morning, it's up to 110/70.

Later – 7:25 p.m.

When I got home, I returned a call to the Chancellor of the Diocese of Raleigh. Someone complained that I had refused to let the Boy Scouts start a troop at St. Catherine's. On the contrary, I welcomed them heartily with the condition that they sign a non-discrimination clause. As it turned out, it was a moot point because there was no room for the troop to meet. The person who schedules our rooms is new on the job, and she didn't appreciate the shortage of space.

I'm also so very grateful for being an American this evening. After my surgery, I can't help but think that if I had been born a Ugandan, for example, I would have been dead long ago. Now, with a very simple procedure, I can live many more years—God willing!

October 24, 2002 – Thursday
Wake Forest, N.C. – 3:45 p.m.
Cloudy – 57 F

Well, the first day back to work from the angioplasty has been wild: staff meeting, spiritual counseling with a parishioner, setting up meetings for next week, doing grocery shopping, stopping at the bank and post office, revising a presentation on the Sacrament of Reconciliation and touring the new rectory with a parishioner.

The most exciting thing of this morning, however, was visiting with Erik, who will be heading up our new Full Stewardship effort. It is so wonderful to have such excellent leaders who are filled with the Spirit in our parish. It makes the headaches much more bearable. We're aiming to have our first planning meeting with our group of seven next week. We will probably set up our yearly goal at that time. Then we can figure out the strategies to get to the goal.

The "fly in the ointment" is that some parishioners, none of whom have come to me to discuss it, have complained to the Diocese of Raleigh, claiming that I won't let the Boy Scouts form a troop at St. Catherine's. I told the vicar general that that is untrue. In fact, I invited the Boy Scouts to form a troop—before I learned we had no room—on the condition that they sign a document saying that they will not discriminate against people. They cannot do this according to their national charter. As I pointed out to the diocese, we have a policy that excludes groups from using our parish facilities that are out of harmony with Catholic beliefs. Because the Boy Scouts have an anti-gay position, in direct contrast to many, many Church documents calling for the respect of human dignity of all persons, we cannot accept them unless they reject their homophobic position. Until then, they may not establish a troop at St. Catherine's.

This evening, I have a counseling session with a deacon candidate, Mass and a presentation to second grade parents whose children are studying to make their First Reconciliation in the winter and First Holy Communion in the spring.

In short, I am living my priesthood to the fullest!

October 25, 2002 – Friday
Wake Forest, N.C. – 10:10 p.m.
Cloudy – 60s F

My workday ended yesterday with a parishioner coming to visit me about my homilies. He had suggestions on how they could be better. Such an interaction is not easy to hear, but on the other hand, I am grateful for his visit. After all, one of the things that I am most complimented on is my preaching. It is good to hear some constructive criticism once in a while.

Today, I blessed a new house in Henderson, N.C. The family believes they had a ghost in their last house, which was in a bad neighborhood with lots of robberies of Mexican households. The new place is in the country and much safer. I wish them all the best in their new place.

I also had a nice visit with the Religion Editor of the *News & Observer*. She is doing a special on Catholic growth in North Carolina and she chose St. Catherine of Siena parish as her model. She chose our parish because it's located in Wake Forest, long noted as the bastion of Southern Baptists and the Southeastern Baptist Theological Seminary, formerly Wake Forest College. Though Southern Baptists are still the majority denomination in North Carolina, their percentage is dropping while the proportion of Catholics is rising. I hope the article is a credit to our parish.

This evening, I celebrated Mass for about 21 people who are having a mini-retreat on "Designing Your Own Spirituality." I'll be covering defining spirituality, differentiating spirituality from religion, listing signs of healthy vs. unhealthy spirituality, and showing how, when viewed with the right lens, all facets of life can be spiritual. Tomorrow, we'll meet from 9:00 a.m. to around 1:30 p.m., or so.

As I write this note this evening, I'm feeling low. I don't know if I'm entering a period of darkness or desert or what. Usually in the fall and spring, November and May to be specific, I go into one or two weeks of depression. I think I am just worried about the right-wingers who may try to harm me by their hate. God, help me to trust You more. Protect my parish and myself from evil. Let me always do the best I can in my vocation, and let me touch the hearts of those who are coming to the mini-retreat this weekend. Thank You!

October 26, 2002 – Saturday
Wake Forest, N.C. – 6:55 p.m.
Partly sunny – 67 F

I've just gotten home from church, where I've been since 8:00 a.m. It's been a wonderful day filled with many things that have nourished my spirit. However, I'm ready to collapse right now as I only slept about two hours last night due to worry.

The "Designing Your Own Spirituality" retreat went very well, and we had lots of good discussion and food. One person fainted in the hallway after the morning talk, and her son had to come to take her home. We don't know what exactly happened. She believes she got dizzy and then fainted, hitting her head on the floor. She has a pacemaker, but her pulse was fine. I joked with her that she probably was "slain in the Spirit" from my preaching. She liked that.

This weekend, we have nine baptisms. I had five of them today and will have four tomorrow. The 2:30 p.m. baptisms were in Spanish, with about 40 people attending. It was quite a celebration. The three Anglo children who were baptized came with about 50 people. So, the sanctuary was quite a scene from 2:30 p.m. to 3:45 p.m.

I'm preaching on the forgotten third of the Great Commands of Jesus Christ—to love self. Many preachers forget this part of the command.

After Mass this evening, the Welcome Committee hosted a newcomers' dinner with salad, baked ziti and other good things.

I'm going around the house turning the clocks back an hour as it is time to "fall back." I truly need the extra hour of sleep tonight of all nights!

October 27, 2002 – 30th Sunday of Ordinary Time
Wake Forest, N.C. – 6:40 p.m.
Partly sunny – 67 F

I had a wonderful sleep last evening—10 hours' worth. It's amazing what some good sleep can do for a person!

Today, I gave a pep talk after each Mass in English about our parish vision, the Anglo Youth Group and the barbeque they are having next Saturday. Some of the money will be used to send six teenage missionaries to Honduras to help build houses for the poor in our sister parish. I told the people that I thought the idea was classy – very, very classy. They applauded in agreement. After the Masses, the youths sold many tickets.

The Hispanic Youth Group, under the direction of Jesús, is doing great. They now have about 25 members. They are going to decorate some tables in the sanctuary for next weekend with food, candles and photos of deceased family members. This is a Mexican custom associated with the Day of the Dead or All Souls' Day. I'm eager for the Anglos to share in this custom.

The Hispanic community surprised me today. I let a Hispanic woman give a witness talk on her experience in a charismatic conference. After her talk, she called me forward, and the whole community outstretched their arms to give me a blessing. It was very touching. Now, more than ever, I need the warm support of the community. Then, after the Mass in Spanish, a group of *mariachis* showed up unexpectedly to serenade the community as they were leaving Mass. The *mariachi* band was hired by one of the families whose child was baptized at that Mass.

Good news from one of my priest friends: He is leaving a treatment center this coming week and beginning a new life. May God go with him.

October 28, 2002 – Monday – SS Simon & Jude
Wake Forest, N.C. – 9:00 p.m.
Rainy – 60 F

This day has been so healing for me! I am especially thankful that I was able to come to a graceful solution to the Boy Scouts issue. I talked with the Scout leader, Steve, and I told him that the Boy Scouts would be able to set up a troop with the understanding that if they disrespected the human dignity of any person based on how God made them, the parish would immediately revoke its support. This allows the Boy Scouts to function without signing a document of non-discrimination. This way, the boys can gain something from scouting, and I will be upholding the triple love ethic of Jesus Christ by accepting all people, not just heterosexuals, as worthy of respect based on their human dignity. In other words, I will uphold Catholic teaching.

I also met with a young man named Doug today, a person filled with passion and longing to do great things for the Lord. I invited Doug to be part of our Full Stewardship team. In this position, he can meet more people in the parish and contribute to our effort, as well as use the experience to discern the Spirit in his life.

This evening, the Documents of Vatican II class discussed *Dei Verbum*, (The Document on Divine Revelation). We had about 18 people attending, and we had great discussion.

As the day closes, I thank God for all His blessings.

October 30, 2002 – Wednesday
Wake Forest, N.C. – 8:55 p.m.
Cloudy – 50s F

This has been a wonderful day – low-key and relaxing.

I started off by buying several notebooks for my journals and other writings at Staples. The clerk, also from Wake Forest, said that there is talk about building a Staples store in our town. That would be super!

I then bought a house blessing plaque for the new rectory. It features the Sacred Heart with this House Blessing:

> God bless the corners of this house,
> > And the lintel blest;
> And bless the hearth and bless the board
> > And bless each place of rest;
> And bless each door that opens wide
> > To stranger as to kin;
> And bless each crystal window pane
> > That lets the starlight in;
> And bless the rooftree overhead
> > And every sturdy wall,
> The peace of man, the peace of God,
> > The peace of love on all.

I also bought a couple of books that I'm eager to read. The first is *Christmas Presence: Twelve Gifts That Were More Than They Seemed*, edited by Gregory F. Augustine Pierce (ACTA Publications, 2002). It contains 12 Christmas stories. As a child of Christmas, I love Christmas stories for personal nourishment. And as a priest, I am always looking for good stories to enhance my preaching.

The second book is called *Father Mychal Judge: An Authentic American Hero* (Paulist Press, 2002). The subject of the book was a Franciscan priest in New York City who gave his life in the New York tragedy of September 11, 2001. I'm especially looking forward to reading about how Fr. Judge dealt with his gay identity and alcoholism.

The author is Dr. Michael Ford, who wrote *The Wounded Prophet: A Portrait of Henri J.M. Nouwen,* the excellent book about the life of the late Fr. Henri Nouwen, a priest and one of the most prolific and influential Catholic spiritual writers of the 20th Century.

This evening, the Full Stewardship Committee met for the first time. I think Erik will be a super leader. The group set our financial target: $1.7 million per year in parishioner giving. This is doable. It will take a lot of work, but we will accomplish it. God will be with us. God give us strength to make this dream a reality.

October 31, 2002 – Thursday – Halloween
Wake Forest, N.C. – 5:25 p.m.
Cloudy – 54 F

Halloween is upon us. This is the first year that I have not decorated a jack-o'-lantern. I just didn't have the energy, and besides, I have to leave the trick-or-treaters to celebrate the Vigil Mass of All Saints' Day at 7:00 p.m. I'll be able to give out treats to the youngest trick-or-treaters and after Mass, I'll be able to catch the older kids. I hate to disappoint those who will arrive to find a dark house, even if it's only for an hour or so.

I have decided to very methodically document the history of the Full Stewardship idea. In time, when we have successfully completed our project, I will write a book on the subject so that other parishes may benefit from our experience. I am confident that we can pull it off. We do have to be careful, however, that the Diocese of Raleigh personnel are kept informed so they don't feel threatened in any way. At times, it's like walking on eggshells working with some of the people at the Catholic Center. I would like them to feel that they are part of this incredible adventure and not outsiders.

Bob Neal says the new rectory should be ready for me to move in around mid-December. Next week, we'll go shopping for lamps and flooring, I believe. The house is 2,050 square feet, I learned today. Bob said that he's very pleased at how the house is coming along, and so am I. He mentioned that he's very pleased with the color of the siding, ivy green with cream-colored trim. He wasn't sure how it would look, as it's hard to tell from just a little swatch, but now he loves it. He's received many compliments from people who love the color.

This morning, I took two of our parishioners, Joe and Fausto, with our school's director, to visit selected sites for playgrounds. We're going to clear a field on the West Campus as a temporary playfield for our children. Eventually, I imagine it will be a huge parking lot for our new sanctuary and office building. It will serve as a play area until we get our official soccer/baseball field done. We also chose an area near the Trinity Center that we will make into an enclosed play area for preschoolers.

All in all, it was a very productive day.

Now, I am busy working on my upcoming weekend homily about humility and how we will all be passing away. I'm going to talk about the origins of the Mexican celebration of *El Día de los Muertos* or Day of the Dead (All Souls' Day). I'm eager to see the *Altar de los Muertos*, the Altar of the Dead that the Hispanic Youth Group will set up tomorrow! It will be a wonderful "visual aid" for a most interesting homily for the Anglos.

NOVEMBER 2002

November 2, 2002 – Saturday – All Souls' Day
Wake Forest, N.C. – 7:55 p.m.
Sunny – 54 F

Today was a picture-perfect kind of fall day—blue skies with plenty of sunshine, crisp and trees turning every shade of gold and red and orange.

Great news! John has successfully negotiated with EUE Screen Gems, and Wray, attorney and St. Catherine Pastoral Council Chair, received a copy of the "letter of intent" to begin production of *Manic Ride* on February 2003. I don't yet know the details, but I should learn more on Monday.

This morning, I met Bob at Home Depot to decide on various items for the new rectory. We picked out the color of the wall paint (soft yellow), the countertop for the kitchen, the refrigerator and microwave, and the lighting and ceiling fans. That rectory is going to be awesome!

This afternoon, I noticed someone mowing the field on the West Campus, getting it ready to turn it into a temporary playground. I'm sure the kids will appreciate it and many childhood memories will be made there.

This evening, I gave positive strokes to some St. Catherine youth. The school children made wonderful posters of different saints they have been studying for All Saints' Day. The Visions Youth Group worked all day today preparing for their barbeque this evening to raise money, in part, to send six teenaged missionaries to our sister parish in San Pedro Sula, Honduras during spring break. And the Hispanic Youth Group did a fabulous job designing the *Altar de Muertos*. What an energetic place St. Catherine's is!

November 3, 2002 – 31st Sunday in O.T.
Wake Forest, N.C. – 7:00 p.m.
Sunny – 54 F

I write this note at the end of an excellent day. The weather was perfect, and the Masses went very well. The people loved hearing about the Aztec custom of honoring the dead and how the Spanish priests in Mexico helped the newly Christianized people to transform the custom into a Christian one. The people loved the *Altar de Muertos* that the Hispanic Youth Group put up.

The barbeque dinner hosted by the Visions Youth Group went well. I got many compliments on it. And people are complimenting the new rectory, especially the color—ivy green with cream trim.

This afternoon, after taking a nap, I was able to prepare for my Vatican II class and write my Pastor's Corner for both the English and Spanish bulletins. Now I'm going to make myself a little dinner and sit and watch *Home Alone 4* on TV. I need a relaxing evening!

November 4, 2002 – Monday – St. Charles Borromeo
Wake Forest, N.C. – 4:30 p.m.
Partly sunny – 61 F

There were about 80 people for the Anointing Mass this morning. Some of them were not members of our parish, but they tend to show up for unusual things. How they hear about such events is beyond me. We had a little lunch of tomato soup, chips and sandwiches. I sat with some Hispanic women and was able to practice my Spanish with a woman from Costa Rica who did not know any English.

The politicians are in frenzied today, the day before Election Day. The U.S. House and Senate are both up for grabs. Will the voters keep the Senate in Democratic hands and the House in Republican hands? What will happen to our country if the Republicans take over both houses of Congress with a Republican president? Exciting things are happening with the movie, *Manic Ride*. John is designing the new website, and we should be receiving some money soon. St. Catherine's will be getting 10 percent of the initial sale. Now, I'll have to begin practicing my lines!

November 5, 2002 – Tuesday – Election Day
Wake Forest, NC – 5:25 p.m.
Rainy – 50 F

As I write this, it's rainy and very chilly outside, the kind of chill that goes to the bone. In my heart, however, I have plenty of joy.

Jeff and Anne got back safe and sound from their Ugandan adventure. Jeff lost eight pounds. Anne had an infestation of white-winged bugs one night in her room, but she survived. I can hardly wait to hear all the stories they have to tell! Jeff says that they complemented each other very well. Jeff was better on the camcorder and cameras, while Anne did a super job taking notes.

Today, I received the letter of intent to make the movie, *Manic Ride.* EUE Screen Gems will be in charge of production, while First Look Media will be in charge of distribution. The production start date is February 1, 2003. Partnerships will be formed with the Depression & Bipolar Support Alliance (DBSA) and the North Carolina and New York film commissions. A sponsorship has been entered into with Eli Lilly, and many other investment groups and other companies will be brought on board to help fund the enterprise. This is so exciting!

This evening after Mass and the Liturgy Committee meeting, I look forward to spending a relaxing evening finishing my homily in Spanish and watching the election results. Perhaps I'll have some popcorn.

November 6, 2002 – Wednesday
Wake Forest, N.C. – 7:50 p.m.
Partly sunny – 50s F

Well, the Republicans captured the U.S. House of Representatives and the Senate. We're stuck with Elizabeth Dole, who will be the new Senator from North Carolina. She has got to be better than Jesse Helms, who is retiring.

The marijuana issues all failed, but it was amazing that the initiatives had even the support they did have. I imagine that someday down the line there will be legalized marijuana in the land.

Today, I was up at 4:30 a.m. and could not go back to sleep. I'm exhausted this evening, as I was at the CARA conference all day at St. Michael's in Cary. The presenter is a sociologist and very sharp. We had lunch together. I did a short presentation on registering Hispanics in the parish setting, and it went well. My favorite presentation was by my friend

Fr. Shay from St. Raphael's. He gave us a handout of various Hispanic customs that can be used in liturgy. I especially liked the explanation of the *piñata*.

November 7, 2002 – Thursday
Wake Forest, NC – 9:00 p.m.
Partly sunny – 54 F

When I began this day, I had a feeling that it would be special. Now that it is almost over, I can say that feeling came true.

The first good thing that happened to me this morning was finding a copy of a beautiful letter that the vicar general of our diocese wrote to a complaining parishioner. The complainers are the type that complain as a matter of course. Msgr. Shugrue told them that I am doing wonderful work at St. Catherine's and explained to them why I do what I do. The letter was obviously not a slap-dash kind of thing. It reflected much wisdom and prudence.

I spent most of the day at St. Michael the Archangel in Cary with the priests, deacons and pastoral administrators of the Diocese of Raleigh. We listened to an expert in liturgy from Washington, D.C. who talked about the new liturgical reforms. We have agreed that nothing will be started until after Christmas.

I especially enjoyed lunch, sitting between Shay from St. Raphael's and *mi amigo*, Arturo. We had a great conversation and laughed a lot. Arturo is planning on coming to my new rectory when it opens. I told him I'm naming the guestroom the Padre Arturo Room, as he is always the first guest in any place I go to. Shay is a delightful Jesuit who is very easy to talk to. We'll be having lunch one of these days.

When the conference was only in its first half hour, I got called out to administer the Sacrament of the Sick to a man dying at Rex Cancer Center. His daughter-in-law goes to St. Catherine's. He's baptized but not Catholic. His breathing was labored, and he was getting oxygen.

Yesterday, two men asked me for financial help, a cousin in prison and a friend, so I was hoping that I could get some money. This evening when

I went to church to celebrate Mass, there was a check for $905 for me in my mailbox. The Lord works in mysterious ways!

There was also a strange note attached to one of the desk lamps in my office wishing me the best in my "upcoming nuptials." Who knows what that means!

Before Mass this evening, a young man named Brad talked with me about going to the missions. I sense a very definite Church vocation in him to serve God. Perhaps the Lord is calling him to be a diocesan priest, but perhaps he's being called to be a missionary. I will work closely with him. I suggested that he get some experience with the Maryknoll missionaries, and he thought that would be a good idea.

Finally, after Mass this evening, I talked to the Home & School Association group. I got so energized talking about my Full Stewardship dream that I am all wound up as I write this. What a great day, and what gratitude I have for my many blessings!

November 8, 2002 – Friday
Wake Forest, N.C. – 9:15 p.m.
Sunny – 54 F

I learned what the wedding bell on my lamp means. Apparently, our development director was at the *Wake Weekly* the other day, and the staff was talking about me leaving St. Catherine's to get married! How on earth that rumor started is totally beyond me.

Today, I had a great meeting with two people from Southlight, a chemical dependency organization that has six divisions. Agnes (a member of our parish) and a man named David and I got together to discuss what we could do for the Hispanic members of our parish. My recommendation is that we do education. Many Hispanic men come to me to write a *juramento*, a document promising not to take a drink for a period of time. It is similar to the old Irish "pledge." I think we could do some workshops, as well as have Spanish brochures and such on the signs and symptoms of alcoholism, where the Spanish-speaking AA meetings are.

I also visited a 27-year-old man named Chris. He is the young man who got hit by a van downtown while on the sidewalk. The van had been hit by another vehicle and careened into Chris, throwing him into some bushes in front of a church. Chris and I got to laughing as we saw this as a rather dramatic "kick in the butt" to get his life together. After some years gone from the Church, Chris will now be returning. I'm looking forward to welcoming him back. Fortunately for Chris, he has only a fractured pelvis that will heal, and his wife is a rehab R.N.

I visited Teresa at Raleigh Community Hospital today. She had a little stroke. Teresa is one of our Eucharistic ministers, and I helped her and her husband celebrate their 50th wedding anniversary last Christmastime.

I got a call today from Yonat, the religion editor of the *News & Observer*. She is sending a photographer to our parish on Sunday to take photos of me baptizing Hispanic babies. I have five baptisms this weekend, two of them at the Mass in Spanish. Yonat said the article would run on Sunday, November 24th. It will feature St. Catherine's and the irony of this fast-growing parish being in Wake Forest, site of the rightwing Southeastern Baptist Theological Seminary.

Yesterday, the realtor put up a "For rent or sale" sign in my yard. She knows that I won't be out of here until mid-December. I have begun packing books.

November 10, 2002 – 32nd Sunday of Ordinary Time
Wake Forest, N.C. – 9:00 p.m.
Sunny – 74 F

This has been one of the most beautiful weekends I have ever seen weather-wise. The sun has been shining, and the trees are magnificent in their fall colors of red and gold and orange and yellow and brown. The temperatures have been great.

Today, I learned that the Aztec dancers that we had last year for the Our Lady of Guadalupe festivities at St. Catherine's would be back this year. Even more exciting is that they are going to teach a group of our Hispanic youth to be such dancers. In the future, we will be able to have our own dancers without having to rely on outsiders.

Today, some of the Hispanic community asked me for my opinion on whether or not the Aztec dancers should be allowed inside the sanctuary to dance. The issue was that some of the people don't like the fact that some of the dancers wear very little clothing. "What is your opinion, Padre?" they asked. I said that God made us naked, and I don't see anything wrong with having the dancers. After all, they are covered in all the sensitive places. The group applauded, for that group was all for letting in the dancers.

The Hispanic Youth Group is also planning many new projects. One will focus on the Epiphany, the Feast of the Three Kings. In many Latin American countries, this is a very big holiday, a day when children get presents.

Today, a staff photographer from the *News & Observer*, a friendly young man named Ethan, came to St. Catherine's to do photos at our Mass in Spanish. He will be back next week to take some more photos.

I enjoyed talking with our missionaries, Jeff and Anne, this weekend. They have wonderful adventures to share from their Ugandan trip. They'll be telling the whole community at all the Masses of November 23rd and 24th.

I also learned today that the gentleman I anointed the other day died peacefully in his sleep. I also learned that he had a long history of being a bootlegger and a member of the mob. When he was asked about if he ever bootlegged in North Carolina, he replied, "only for the seminary in Wake Forest." I get a big kick out of that!

I continue to pack. I believe the move will be pretty easy. I have never had to move such a short distance before!

November 12, 2002 – Wednesday
Wake Forest, N.C. – 9:00 p.m.
Off and on rain – 55 F

I'm getting a sore throat and have been a bit depressed today. There's nothing specific that I'm depressed about, just experiencing fleeting feelings of impending doom. On the other hand, it's been a good day, with no meetings except for the one this evening with Jeff and Anne about their experiences in Uganda.

We viewed some of their photos that came out great. They told me about the change in pastors at our sister parish in Muduuma. I'm thinking that it's time to change our sister parish relationship to maybe a parish in the Arua Diocese. We have done so much for Muduuma parish. Now it's time to help someone else. They agreed that the Arua Diocese is a very worthy place to help.

Jeff and Anne are planning on speaking at all the Masses the weekend after next. They plan on doing a slideshow for the people. I think everyone will be very happy to hear of their experiences.

November 14, 2002 – Thursday
Wake Forest, N.C. – 9:12 p.m.
Sunny – 64 F

As I write this, I am exhausted from a grueling day of nonstop activities!

Today, I told the story of St. Meinrad to the Kindergarten class, picked up my new glasses, had a great meeting with my spiritual director and attended a Deanery meeting this evening at Cardinal Gibbons High School. I got to know Fr. Mel from St. Eugene's better. He is a very easy person with which to talk.

The highlight of the day, however, was my meeting with Debbie from the diocese. We went to Rock-Ola Café for lunch, and I told her of our dream for St. Catherine's to become a Full Stewardship parish. I told her of our goal, our committee, our preliminary work, some initial strategies and how the Diocese of Raleigh can assist us in making the dream a reality. The meeting went well, and I went back to St. Catherine's on a cloud. When I returned, everyone was asking how the meeting went, and all told me they had been praying for me. I guess I didn't realize how fully the staff understood the importance of this meeting. I am convinced that we will accomplish what we set out to achieve.

I have been fighting off a sore throat for the last two days. It appears that regular ibuprofen plus gargling with salt water is working. I would hate to think of what would happen if I should get laryngitis on a weekend with five Masses!

November 15, 2002 – Friday – St. Albert the Great
Wake Forest, N.C. – 7:25 p.m.
Sunny – 64 F

Today was a beautiful fall day. It was the kind of day that lifts one's spirits.

Today was an "art day" for me. Not only did I pick up some artwork that I had framed by some parishioners, but I also bought two calendars that I'll use for framing. One is an Americana calendar with the works of Charles Wysocki, and the other is the 2003 Lang Folk Art Calendar by Linda Nelson Stocks.

Later, I visited two people in the hospital, and then went out to lunch with Wray at the Rock-Ola Café near his office. It appears that by Monday, we should have the final word on the movie.

November 16, 2002 – Saturday
Wake Forest, N.C. – 8:00 p.m.
Rainy – 60 F

Some of the most important things I learn come from people speaking what appears at the time to be random thoughts. For example, at the CARA conference on Hispanic ministry that I attended last week, Shay was talking about how scared he used to be to converse in Spanish on the telephone. The vivid way he described this fear hit the nail on the head for me, as I feel that way right now. But after identifying this as a problem that others have faced and conquered, I am not so fearful of talking on the phone to someone who speaks only Spanish. I love how God puts gems in my life just when I need them.

Today, I helped at St. Andrew's in Apex, N.C. with their First Reconciliation Service. There were around 200 children making their First Reconciliation.

This afternoon, Ethan from the *News & Observer* came to photograph a baptism I performed at St. Catherine's. He has a great personality, someone with whom I connect very easily. I told him as much, and he told me the feeling was mutual. Tomorrow, I'm showing him some of my photography of the Hispanic community at St. Catherine's. I took some of it at the Hispanic Safety Fair last year, and others at last year's Our Lady of Guadalupe festival at St. Catherine's.

November 17, 2002 – 33rd Sunday in O.T.
Wake Forest, N.C. – 6:45 p.m.
Rainy – 54 F

Because of a bad cold with a hacking cough, I took many pills to get through the morning. Fortunately, I got through four Masses and a baptism in fine shape. Ethan came to the 10:30 a.m. Mass to take photos, and Yonat, the religion editor of the *News & Observer,* came to the Mass in Spanish.

This week, I told the *Dream Catcher* story. The moral of the story is that we all have a dream, but sometimes we let time get away from ourselves. We let the dream die. But the Holy Spirit often sends wind through wind chimes to remind us of our dreams. We are called to be good stewards, to make the most of our lives, to live our dreams. I think the people liked the story and the message.

I have just finished my last lesson plan for the Documents of Vatican II adult education series. Now, I'll begin preparing for the *Adventures in American Catholic Spirituality* series for the spring.

November 19, 2002 – Tuesday
Wake Forest, N.C. – 8:50 p.m.
Sunny – 60 F

Dad called this morning to let me know that Aunt Bobbie died at 2:00 a.m. She was at home, and she died in Uncle Jim's arms. They had been married for 48 years. I have made plans to go home Thursday for the evening visiting hours and will be there to lead the funeral at Holy Family Church in Stow, Ohio on Friday morning. I'll return on Friday evening to Raleigh. Fortunately, Continental Airlines gave me a "compassionate rate."

November 20, 2002 – Wednesday
Wake Forest, N.C. – 8:20 p.m.
Sunny – 60 F

I have been battling a cold for the last few days, and my energy is very low. I have zero appetite. My spirits are flagging also. It'll be a great challenge to be "on" for my family tomorrow and Friday in Ohio as I lead the wake service and funeral for my aunt. With God's help, though, I'm sure I'll pull through.

The bishop called me today and told me that E, the woman who attempts to destroy priests, continues to stir up hatred. Hatred, especially from those who believe they are morally superior to others, is very difficult for me. Hatred is so anti-Christ that it penetrates the core of my being. God, if You are testing me, please be sure to give me enough strength to meet the challenge! Thanks!

We had the second meeting of the Full Stewardship Committee this evening. We have decided that to get $1.7 million, we need to set our unannounced goal as $2 million. We are closing in on building "the case." When that is done, we will design a clear brochure explaining the concept of Full Stewardship and how the people can get onboard. With my low energy right now, it's hard to imagine how we'll accomplish our task. But, I believe the Holy Spirit will guide us through this.

November 23, 2002 – Saturday
Wake Forest, N.C. – 10:25 a.m.
Sunny – 54 F

It's so good to be at home this morning in my cozy house after my wild experiences these past few days.

The funeral for Aunt Bobbie went very well. Fr. Mike Ausperk concelebrated the Mass at Holy Family Church in Stow, Ohio and both he, and the new administrator of Holy Family, came to the funeral home the evening before to give condolences. It was good to see the family once again and see my folks' new condo in Stow.

After the funeral, we went to Northfield for the burial. The first snow-fall of the year began in earnest while I was doing the rite of committal. A bagpiper played several tunes in the snowstorm, and the wind was very strong. Because I was afraid that the snowstorm would make my plane late leaving Cleveland, thus making me miss my connecting flight in Newark, N.J., I opted to rent a car and drive to North Carolina.

The drive back was an adventure indeed. The snow, fog and strong winds dogged me through the mountains of West Virginia into Virginia. Salt trucks were out salting the mountain roads in West Virginia. There was only a small part of the journey where snow was sticking on the pave-ment. The pines glistened with new-falling snow and were quite beautiful.

By the time I got to North Carolina, the roads were dry as a bone. Un-fortunately, there was a major accident in Greensboro, N.C., so the traffic crawled at a snail's pace for about 40 minutes. I don't think I have ever gone through Greensboro without having a hassle of backed-up traffic!

Thanks be to God, I got back to Wake Forest around 9:45 p.m. safe and sound. Needless to say, I slept like a log all night!

This morning, I met Anne and Jeff, who went to Uganda, at church at 8:00 a.m. They went through their slide presentation, which is excel-lent. I told them that this presentation would set the standard for all future missionary reports at St. Catherine's. Now, I'm looking forward to learning how to do PowerPoint myself so that I can put things together in this way.

November 24, 2002 – Sunday – Feast of Christ the King
Wake Forest, N.C. – 6:45 p.m.
Sunny – 60 F

Jeff and Anne's slide presentation on their trip to Uganda went very well. I'm sure everyone appreciated it, and I'm also sure that parents will use this experience to remind their children to be grateful for all they have, for much of the world will go to bed hungry tonight.

On this last Sunday of the liturgical year, Ethan came to take more photos for the *News & Observer* story, and Religion Editor Yonat came to let me know the story should appear in next Sunday's paper. She said that it would be about the growth of Wake Forest, not just about St. Catherine's. I'm looking forward to reading the story.

The Internet is truly fascinating to me, and I'm always amazed at what it can produce. This evening, for example, I was thinking of next week's homily. The first reading of Year B features Isaiah telling us that God is like a potter, and we are the clay (Is 64:7). I thought I'd like to use the teacup story that I remember reading some time ago, but I was not able to find it. Thinking it would be a slim chance, I typed in "teacup story" on the Internet, and believe it or not, the teacup story appeared several times! What a marvelous world we have thanks to technology.

November 28, 2002 – Thanksgiving Day
Wake Forest, N.C. – 5:45 p.m.
Sunny – 40 F

What a wonderful Thanksgiving Day I am having today! I was going to go to Ohio to be with family, but a snowstorm in West Virginia and Ohio dashed those plans. It's just as well, for now I have three whole uninterrupted days to do whatever I want. What an incredible treat that is! Today, I packed 20 boxes for my approaching move to the new rectory.

The other day, Bob Neal and I went shopping for the new rectory. We got a beautiful stained glass lamp for over the dining room table and ordered carpet (bark color) and tile for the kitchen, bathrooms and bonus room (yellowish tint). The house will be very warm, indeed. I saw a few wonderful stained-glass lamps at Lowe's Home Improvement. I'm thinking of going back and buying at least one for myself.

The principal search goes on. We have decided to expand our search to Boston and New York and to put an ad in the *National Catholic Reporter*. Though we have at least one candidate that would likely be very good, we want to be sure that we get the very best we can.

Monday, I visited Fr. Matt in Wilmington to interview him for a vocation article for the *North Carolina Catholic*. I can't believe that I forgot to take his photograph! Fortunately, the secretary of St. Mark's had a photo, which she emailed to me.

November 29, 2002 – Friday
Wake Forest, N.C. – 8:35 p.m.
Sunny – 54 F

Sue Byrne died during the night, so I met Tommy, her husband of 63 years, at Bright's Funeral Home. Tommy and Sue were among the original St. Catherine couples. In fact, Tommy, a former New York Yankees pitcher, was a member of the parish before it even was a parish. The funeral will be on Monday, and it should be quite large. This evening, two of Tommy's sons dropped by my house and asked if I would invite the bishop and the vocation director to be at the funeral, too. Naturally, I said yes. I asked Rev. Dr. Tom Jackson, Pastor of Wake Forest Baptist Church, to be the homilist. He's a friend of mine and of the Byrne family.

Tommy and Sue donated the land on which the new rectory is located. Tommy was once the Mayor of Wake Forest, and Sue was affectionately known as "Mama Sue" to many people. What very lovely people!

I also talked with Jay, a former NC State University student of mine. Jay is just finishing his undergraduate degree from the University of Virginia, and is now getting ready to apply to law schools. I'm going to write a letter of recommendation for him. Of all my NCSU students, Jay definitely stands out as one of my best. It's always a pleasure to write letters for outstanding students.

November 30, 2002 – Saturday
Wake Forest, N.C. – 9:25 p.m.
Sunny – 60 F

This is the last day of November and the first day of the new liturgical year, Weekdays Year 1, and Sundays Cycle B. We'll be hearing from Mark now instead of Matthew. Naturally, on this first day of Advent, we hear from my favorite prophet, Isaiah who talks today about God as potter and us as clay.

The Mass this evening was pretty much packed. In addition to having the Blessing of the Advent Wreath, we also had a baptism in English and two Presentations in the Temple of twin boys, Raul and Benjamin.

Despite all the activity at Mass, I was able to get through the service in one hour.

Following Mass, I went to Raleigh Community Hospital to visit a parishioner who the physicians suspect might have pancreatic cancer. I visited with him and his family, and I celebrated the Sacrament of the Sick with him. The final diagnosis won't come in till Wednesday when the biopsy comes back. We can only pray for the best.

All in all, it's been a good month, but I'm looking forward to December, the month I move into the new rectory.

DECEMBER 2002

December 1, 2002 – First Sunday of Advent
Wake Forest, N.C. – 6:25 p.m.
Sunny – 42 F

December has arrived big time. Today, the *News & Observer* had a big photo of me baptizing a baby on the front page of the paper, and a large and well-written article followed. The thrust of the article was about how the Southern Baptists are declining in percentage in North Carolina and the Triangle, while Roman Catholics are gaining in percentage. The article used statistics from the Glenmary Research Center. It showed that in the Triangle, from 1971 to 2000, Southern Baptists went from 23.8 percent to 13-14 percent of the population; Methodists went from 9.81 percent to 6.75 percent, while Roman Catholics went from 2.5 percent to 6.67 percent. (The Triangle includes Chatham, Durham, Franklin, Johnston, Orange and Wake counties.)

The article focuses on Wake Forest. It talks about how St. Catherine of Siena is the largest congregation in town with over 4,300 registered members. It talks about how we have five Masses each weekend, four in English and one in Spanish, and how people have to watch Mass on TV at the 10:30 a.m. Mass because we cannot accommodate everyone in the 503-seat sanctuary.

The article also shows that other non-Baptist, non-Methodist groups are also growing at a rapid rate including the Lutherans, Mormons and Presbyterians. The article noted that two of the fastest-growing Southern Baptist congregations deliberately leave the word "Baptist" out of their literature or formal names. It appears that many people are turned off by the Baptist label, so to gain members, some congregations distance themselves from that name.

I'm sending the religion editor a note of thanks for this well-written article.

Today, the weather changed dramatically. The high today is only supposed to be 42 degrees. That's okay with me, for I usually associate December with cold weather.

Jay, a student I taught at North Carolina State University, came to visit me after my Mass in Spanish today. He is currently finishing up his bachelor's degree in government and psychology from the University of

Virginia. I'll write him a recommendation letter for law school. Jay hopes to make a career in corporate law and politics. Because of his deep passion, clarity of vision and good looks, I foresee a bright future for him.

December 3, 2002 – Tuesday
Wake Forest, N.C. – 9:05 p.m.
Sunny day – 46 F

As I write this, it's becoming increasingly cold outside. Tomorrow, there's supposed to be an ice storm coming through. I am praying it comes, for I could use a full day off. As it stands, we're supposed to have our parish Advent Reconciliation Service tomorrow evening. It would be great if we could cancel it – the people could go next Tuesday to St. Raphael's.

Yesterday, we had the funeral for "Mama Sue" as she was affectionately known. It was quite a large funeral. I was the celebrant, and Rev. Dr. Tom Jackson, Pastor of Wake Forest Baptist Church, was the homilist. Tom is a dear friend of the Byrne family, and he did a wonderful job. I like Tom very much and consider him a good friend. My new rectory is in his neighborhood. We also had Fr. Michael Clay, vocation director for our diocese, Msgr. Jim Jones of New Bern, N.C., and Fr. Des Keenan, former Vicar for Hispanic Ministry for our diocese, as concelebrants.

A bagpiper provided music in the old Wake Forest Town Cemetery. Sue is buried near people who died in the 1880s.

While we were having the post-burial luncheon provided by our parish Comfort Committee, I was called out to talk with three young men from Colombia—Eduardo, Juan Carlos and Hector. They had come to our church to pray, having learned an hour earlier that their mother had died. I will be celebrating the Mass in Spanish for her this coming Sunday.

This morning, I went with a parishioner to visit two of her aunts who are both in their 90s. They live in the family home that was built in 1811! Civil War Union General William Tecumseh Sherman's men General en camped on the land. At that time, the homestead had over 1,000 acres. Sherman himself is said to have slept in the house. The house is magnificent and filled with antiques. There are fireplaces in each room and beautiful carved wood everywhere. It has two kitchens and a greenhouse room. I was most fascinated with the stairway that wound up to another floor where the "birthing room" was located. Though the two elderly women are Baptists, I celebrated the Sacrament of the Sick with them. Before I anointed them, however, they wanted assurance that the blessing would not turn them into Catholics! I assured them that they'd still be Baptists after the blessing.

Today, I ate at The Forks Cafeteria twice. The first time was for lunch with the Wake Forest Ministerial Association. We had a lively discussion on "Defensive Ministry" among other topics. The group assembled was composed of the usual—John from the Presbyterian Church, Gayla from the Methodist Church, Tom from Wake Forest Baptist Church, and Larry from Ridgecrest Baptist Church. I told Gayla how I sang her praises the other day to the Bright family. She is a wonderful addition to our community. Agnes, a member of my congregation, also joined us.

Then, this evening, it was back to The Forks Cafeteria for the annual Wake Forest Christmas Community Dinner. I gave the invocation and the benediction and sat next to a town planner, Agnes, who is into drums. Vivian, the mayor, was also at my table as well as some other community big shots. Part of one of the choirs of Friendship Chapel Baptist Church provided wonderful music for the evening.

December 4, 2002 – Wednesday
Wake Forest, N.C. – 9:20 p.m.
Winter Storm – 32 F

Snow and freezing rain and sleet have all appeared on the scene this afternoon. The governor has asked North Carolinians to avoid going out on the roads unless absolutely necessary. This morning, I cancelled our Advent Reconciliation Service to avoid anyone getting in an accident. It was a treat to have a whole day off! I'm hoping that tomorrow will be a day off also. I'm using the time for reading, packing and getting my Christmas card envelopes ready.

December 5, 2002 – Thursday
Wake Forest, N.C. – 6:30 p.m.
Wintry day: snow and ice – 35 F

I write this note by the light of a lantern in my living room, for my section of town has been without electricity since around midnight due to a fierce ice storm. The fire in the fireplace is keeping me warm, and I have scented candles glowing.

Everything has been cancelled at the church due to the lack of electricity, and school is cancelled tomorrow.

A number of trees have fallen down, knocking out power lines and blocking roads. Though there was some snow—giant, magnificently beautiful flakes—the real problem has been the ice. The trees and bushes, though, are incredibly beautiful. It's as if the world has turned into a magical winter fairyland. The pines and ornamental grasses and bushes glisten with ice. Even this afternoon, the ice has not melted.

Much of the day I packed for my upcoming move. I had coffee and soup heated on the log fire. For some reason, I have had a tremendous appetite all day today.

After packing, I celebrated Mass on my coffee table in front of the fire. Gracing the "altar" were fresh flowers I got at Kroger's the other day—white chrysanthemums, baby's breath, white carnations and some red flowers whose name I do not know—with orange candles and an oil lantern.

Later in the afternoon and evening, I have been reading *The Other Side of the Mountain: The End of the Journey (Journals of Thomas Merton) Volume Seven, 1967-1968*. I truly LOVE reading journals and learning how people "do life." How grateful I am that the Holy Spirit inspires some people to write journals.

In this volume of Merton's journal, the last before his death in Bangkok, he is living in a hermitage on the grounds of The Abbey of Gethsemani in Kentucky. He had become tired of the monastic life, and finally received permission to be a hermit, though remaining a Trappist monk.

I am amazed that he shared some of the same problems I have encountered even though I'm a diocesan priest—an apostolic hermit—while he was a monk hermit. We both relish solitude, yet we both seek to be integrally related and involved in the world.

I see a very common thread in the lives of three of my favorite spiritual writers, all Catholic priests—Thomas Merton, Henri Nouwen, and Andrew Greeley. All of them show a fierce passion about their writing. All love solitude, for it is in solitude that the writer flourishes. Yet each of these three found himself continually getting swamped by the outside world. Each was hounded by interview requests, letters to answer, invitations to give retreats or conferences, and the like. And all knew that they had a need to be social, yet had to get plenty of alone time to do their work as writers.

As I write this reflection by the light of a lantern this icy evening, I pray that perhaps someday, someone—hopefully a parish priest somewhere—will be able to read this journal and find the Spirit talking to him through a soul mate. What a great gift that would be, for me to be able to touch another's life by recording my own life journey as a parish priest and writer!

December 6, 2002 – Friday – St. Nicholas
Wake Forest, N.C. – 6:00 p.m.
Sunny – 35 F

What an incredible place the Triangle is! This morning, the ice was covering all the trees and power lines and bushes. The news media has reported that this is one of the worst ice storms in Triangle history, a "Hurricane Fran with ice." Over a half-million people in the Triangle have been without power. I got my power on around midnight last night, and then it went off again for an hour this morning. The church didn't get power until shortly after noon today.

Trees are down everywhere, including the St. Catherine campus. It truly does look like a post-hurricane scene except with ice. Fortunately, the new rectory did not suffer any damage. Bob says I should be able to move into it the week before Christmas. He should have a more definite date on Monday.

Because of the storm, I have had three unexpected days off. I've been able to do lots of packing, and I got my Christmas letter written. This weekend, I'll get my homily done for December 15th and Pastor's Corners for the next three or four bulletins.

I just finished watching the movie *Erin Brockovich* and loved it! It was my treat for the day.

December 9, 2002 – Monday – Immaculate Conception of Mary
Wake Forest, N.C. – 9:15 p.m.
Sunny – 45 F

I just returned from St. Eugene's in Wendell where I assisted at their Advent Reconciliation Service. Frs. Mel and Charles and Brother Giovanni are wonderful people! I think they are going to add a lot to St. Eugene's.

They forgot to mention that communal reconciliation services are not for in-depth counseling, so many people took forever with the other priests. I was doing six for each of the other priest's one. I also got many Hispanics in my line. I wish I were more fluent with the language. On the other hand, I think they can tell that I love them.

The weekend went very well. We had about the usual number of people despite the recent storm. Some of the people still had no power as of this weekend, and there are hundreds of thousands in North Carolina who still have no electricity. It must be terrible, especially for those with little children.

There are many people, especially Hispanics, who are getting into health trouble because of burning grills inside their homes. Many of them have had to be treated in special breathing chambers to help their bodies get rid of carbon monoxide. There have also been house fires from people trying to warm themselves with kerosene stoves and grills.

On Sunday, after the 12:30 p.m. Mass in Spanish, I was delighted to see many volunteers with chainsaws on the East Campus of St. Catherine's clearing away fallen pine trees. Today, the place looks great – stacks of cut wood sit neatly in different places of the campus. The children now have a safe place to play. There was only minimal loss of trees on the North

Campus where my new rectory is. On the West Campus, the roof of a storage shed was destroyed, but the log cabin is in fine shape.

Today, I went to visit a parishioner named Garry. He has been diagnosed with cancer of the liver, pancreas and stomach. The family has been trying to get him into Duke University Medical Center where a specialist can see him and begin treatment. Because Durham has been hit so hard, Duke's discharges have slowed down, thus making admissions fewer.

As I end this day, I pray for the strength to deal with the city of Wake Forest. We have been waiting since January 11th for a permit to finish our parking lot. I'm seriously thinking of calling for a prayer vigil outside city hall next week if we do not have a permit by then.

December 10, 2002 – Tuesday
Wake Forest, N.C. – 9:00 p.m.
Cloudy – 30s F

What a wonderful day this has turned out to be! The weather has been very cold, the Seattle kind of cold that chills a person to the bone. But many things have happened during the day to make it a "diamond" instead of a "stone."

All the appointments I had this morning went well, and I was able to do some good. I got all my Christmas cards out. This evening, I learned that we would be able to give the parish staff a Christmas bonus after all. And I learned that our parish financial picture is much brighter than it had appeared last month. Finally, I have all day off tomorrow. Bob and I will go refrigerator shopping at 6:45 a.m. as we're both early birds.

December 12, 2002 – Thursday – Our Lady of Guadalupe
Wake Forest, N.C. – 9:20 p.m.
Sunny – 54 F

The amount of work I have to do before my move is daunting, yet I'm plugging away at it. I have a homily for this coming Sunday, the 4th Sunday of Advent (December 22nd), I have one for Christmas, and I've got a good start on the Feast of the Holy Family (December 29th). I have to get them to my translators so they can have them ready in time for me to practice them.

Yesterday, Bob and I went shopping for a refrigerator at Lowe's Home Improvement. They have such a great selection of lamps and appliances compared to Home Depot. Bob told me to count on Friday, December 20th for my move. Harry and the gang have been alerted and are ready and willing to help.

Today, the drive to the rectory was paved, so now we don't have to go around mud to get into the house. Praise be to God!

Today, I got a couple of small booklets from the Daughters of St. Paul about Thomas Merton and Dorothy Day, two of the people I'm featuring in my "Adventures in American Catholic Spirituality" course in the spring. Even though these booklets are very simple, they are well written. They give me the basics of the lives of the two people, certainly plenty of information for a 90 minute presentation. I'll beef up the presentations with my readings of their autobiographies, journals, and biographies. I'll have more than enough information.

The Maryknoll Sisters have graciously come to my aid by sending me plenty of information on the four women martyrs of El Salvador, two of whom were Maryknoll Sisters. Another was an Ursuline Sister from Cleveland and another was a laywoman from Cleveland. When I visited El Salvador a couple of years ago, I visited a little chapel that was constructed in honor of the four women thanks to the generosity of Cleveland priests and others.

This evening, we had a lively Mass in Spanish for the Feast of Our Lady of Guadalupe. The music team was excellent, and it was wonderful to see so many of our Hispanic Youth Group taking part in the celebrations. The choir and band wore red shirts for the occasion.

December 13, 2002 – Friday – St. Lucy
Wake Forest, N.C. – 8:50 p.m.
Rainy – Low 40s F

All day it's been rainy and cold. I hear, though, it is supposed to be beautiful weather for the coming week—until Friday the 20th, the day I move—and then it's supposed to rain. But that's a whole week off, and the weather people are rarely right that far in advance around here.

I visited Garry at Raleigh Community Hospital today. He has a blood clot in his lung, so now he is in intensive care. He is number one on the waiting list for Duke University Medical Center. The physicians are not starting any chemotherapy on him. They want the Duke oncologists to prescribe a treatment plan.

I myself was at Duke today at the Center for Living for a post-angioplasty checkup. I'm in great shape. My physician, Robert Califf, will be doing a large study on aspirin. There is no definitive answer as to how much a person should take for prevention of strokes, heart attacks, et cetera. Perhaps I'll be part of the study.

This evening, St. Catherine of Siena Catholic School had its annual Christmas pageant and it was beautiful. The costumes and scenery were amazing! We have to work on the sound system, though, as much of the play and music was lost because we couldn't hear what was said. Also, younger brothers and sisters in the audience were noisy at times.

The pope accepted Cardinal Law's resignation today. Perhaps that will help the Boston Archdiocese get on with the healing, after so many instances of sex abuse by priests and the administrators' poor handling of the cases.

December 14, 2002 – Saturday
Wake Forest, N.C. – 8:45 p.m.
Sunny & windy – 54 F

This day brought one thing after another—an interesting day.

It began with me out in the woods gathering pine branches to decorate the centerpiece in front of the altar. While I was doing the decoration, young couples were arriving for the Marriage Prep Day sponsored by the St. Catherine team. Also, members of our Anglo youth group were preparing for people to drive through and leave food for the poor.

I went to the frame shop and picked up a couple of pictures I had framed. They turned out beautifully. One is a gift for our DRE who just received her Master's in Religious Education from Loyola in New Orleans, and the other is for my new rectory. Driving past the rectory, I noticed that some men were putting in a sidewalk. I thanked them for saving as many trees as they possibly could. I learned the carpet is coming in Monday.

At 10:30 a.m., I talked to the marriage prep group about sacraments, especially marriage. It was a very quiet group of 17 couples. Quietness does not necessarily mean they weren't learning. In my years of university teaching, I was often surprised at the great evaluations I got from quiet classes. I falsely interpreted quietness with not enjoying the course.

At 2:00 p.m., I met with a couple having marriage problems. The man was quite scary. Not only was he a big man, his rage was palpable. It was almost as though he had stepped out of an alcoholism textbook. Naturally, he denied trouble with alcoholism and blamed his wife, whom he defines as hopeless, for all the problems they were having. I think their marriage has as much chance as a snowball in hell.

At 3:00 p.m., I had just one Anglo baptism, followed by an hour of Reconciliation and the Vigil Mass. Christmas presents for the poor are pouring in to the church. It's a beautiful sight. Too bad people aren't as generous all through the year as they are at Christmastime.

I'm tired this evening, but I'm looking forward to tomorrow, especially the Our Lady of Guadalupe procession and Aztec dancers. It should be quite a production.

December 15, 2002 – 3rd Sunday of Advent
Wake Forest, N.C. – 3:20 p.m.
Sunny – 54 F

Well, the morning went very well. The Christmas presents for the poor keep pouring in. We had to clear one room for them because there were so many. What a great outpouring of generosity.

The Hispanic community was at church when I arrived this morning. They had been singing *mañanitas* in the sanctuary since 6:00 a.m. as is their custom on this feast.

Before the 12:30 p.m. Mass, we had a wonderful procession around the buildings complete with music and praying of the rosary. For some reason the Aztec dancers did not come, but we did have a new dance troupe who helped us to celebrate. The sanctuary was nearly full for the 12:30 p.m. Mass in Spanish, and many of the people were dressed in native costumes. I didn't go to the fiesta after the Mass as I was too tired after the four Sunday Masses.

I told the story of Our Lady of Guadalupe, patron saint of all the Americas. It is a very powerful story filled with incredibly interesting theological and anthropological highlights.

The Christmas presents continue to pour in at the church for the poor. Even people who are not very involved in stewardship brought presents.

Today, I pointed out all of our ministers who have received degrees or certificates in their ministries. This list includes our DRE, who just received her Master of Religious Education degree, six members of the Hispanic community who received Certificates in Hispanic Pastoral Ministry (a two-year program), six members of the Hispanic community who completed a preaching course and are now known as *Predicadores de la Palabra de Dios en la Vida Diaria* (Preachers of the Word of God in Everyday Life), and two staff members who just completed a Spanish course to better serve the Hispanic community. I'm very proud of all these folks. Their dedication and hard work reflects very well on our parish – a dynamic and vibrant place.

December 16, 2002 – Monday
Wake Forest, N.C. – 8:15 p.m.
Sunny – 60 F

I just returned from the Faith Development Program Christmas pageant. I got some good photos. Christmastime is such a messy time in parish life, messy but wonderful!

In one of the magazines I receive, there was a very simple and profound article called "Three Simple Sentences" by Don M. The man wrote about how these three sentences helped him in his work life. I think they are wonderful for life in general:

1. "I was wrong."

2. "I don't know."
3. "I need help."

What a wonderful world this would be if we could more easily put these into our everyday vocabulary!

December 17, 2002 – Tuesday
Wake Forest, N.C. – 7:55 p.m.
Partly cloudy – 45 F

What a great day this was! It started out with going shopping with Bob for bushes for the front of the rectory. Bob got some type of holly, barberries, a Japanese maple and some junipers. The carpet looks great and so does the screened in porch. I can hardly wait to get in and get settled. It'll be fun to decorate the place!

Last evening, I got a call from my dear friend, David E. in Montana. David was a student of mine at the University of Montana, and he later became my best friend in Montana. It was so good to hear from one of the "magic people" in my life.

Tomorrow, I have the whole day off, and it'll be devoted to finishing packing.

December 18, 2002 – Wednesday
Wake Forest, N.C. – 6:15 p.m.
Sunny – 45 F

I've just celebrated the last Mass in my current home. My next home Mass will be on Friday when I'm in the new rectory. I'm thinking of calling the place the "Pastor's Rectory" to distinguish it from the rectory that we'll have for the parochial vicar(s). If at all possible, I do not want to live with someone else. I need my solitude for reflection, writing and getting back the energy that I spend on people.

I'm exhausted from packing most of the day. But the new house looks beautiful, and the new plants in front of the house look great. The workers have put pine straw all over the front and backyards, so it is very woodsy. The screened in porch is done and looks just great. The house inside will be very easy to decorate.

Tomorrow, I have a staff meeting and staff party during which we'll have lunch, and then I have to go to the bishop's annual Christmas party at his house. Then I have a 7:00 p.m. Mass, after which I'll finish all my packing.

This morning, I got some new decorations for the house—especially for Christmastime. Now the trick will be to find everything I need right away when I get to the new home.

December 19, 2002 – Thursday
Wake Forest, N.C. – 9:00 p.m.
Cloudy with sprinkles – 54 F

As I write this, a thick blanket of fog has settled upon our town, and the temperature has gone up. Tomorrow, my moving day, is supposed to be 62 degrees.

Today was a typical pre-Christmas office day. Some of the staff spent all morning sorting out the mountains of Christmas presents for the poor. The trailer home of one of our large Hispanic families burned to the ground a couple of days ago. We'll announce that at all the Masses this weekend. I'm sure the outpouring will be overwhelming, as it was last year for another family, also with seven kids, who suffered a tragedy.

At noon, the staff and faculty got together for a potluck dinner of ham and turkey and various goodies. I brought macaroni salad. The staff bought me a book of Thomas Kinkade and gave me one of his paintings (*Sunrise*) for the new rectory.

In the afternoon, I went to the bishop's annual Christmas party. I find that the longer I'm a priest, the more I enjoy priest events. My friend Arturo will come to my house on December 26th, and I'll take him and his mother to the airport so they can fly to Colombia. Arturo's mother suffers from a brain tumor, and for some reason it is constricting her throat. It sounds very uncomfortable.

Bob received a "certificate of occupancy" today, so I moved a few things into the house. Harry and Mark brought the plants from the deck of the old house and put them on the new deck. Mark also made us a beautiful crèche to put in front of the altar. I know that the kids especially will be crazy about the crèche. I'm eager to put it up!

This is my last journal entry in the current house, for in the morning, six guys will be here to help me move. It's been a wonderful house, and I pray that the new one will be as wonderful.

December 20, 2002 – Friday
Wake Forest, N.C. – 9:10 p.m.
Rainy to sunny, 64 F

I write this from my new rectory. Thanks be to God! I have been working just about nonstop since 4:00 a.m.

The day started off very rainy but warm. I was able to bring some things to the new rectory wearing only a T-shirt. Later, the sun came out and the temperature went back down. Harry Gammon, Billy McClain, Joe Sendelback, Tom O'Larnic, David Perrotta and Mark Downing all came over to help me move. We did it in two trips. Joe and I went to the new Texas Steakhouse for lunch.

This evening, I blessed the house with a private Mass in front of my huge Christmas tree. I also blessed each room of the house with holy water. I pray that this place will be one of peace and joy and growth and holiness, and that I will flourish here. It is a very beautiful place, and I am so grateful to Bob Neal for building it for us and the Byrne's for giving us the land. This is a very important day for the people of St. Catherine's.

I had better quit now, for I'm ready to collapse!

December 21, 2002 – Saturday
Wake Forest, N.C. – 6:40 p.m.
Sunny – 45 F

I think I was sound asleep last night about 10 seconds after my head hit the pillow. As usual, though, I was up naturally at 5:30 a.m.

Today, a group of three Hispanic painters were at the rectory doing trim and touchup painting here and there. I put on a Spanish CD for them, and then put on 540 AM (a Spanish radio station). It's nice to be able to communicate in Spanish!

The living room and kitchen are both decorated, and the study is coming along great. I should have the study done by Christmas Eve, I think. Getting ready for so many Masses and the move has made me hyper-organized. I even have my spices lined up above the stove in alphabetical order!

I began reading a booklet by Margaret Swedish and Lee Miller called *A Message Too Precious to Be Silenced: The Four U.S. Church Women and the Meaning of Martyrdom* (Washington, D.C.: Religious Task Force on Central America, 1992). It will be very helpful in planning the section I'm doing on these four martyrs in the spring "Adventures in American Catholic Spirituality" course.

Many of the people in the parish know that I have moved, and they are very impressed that I have the windows decorated with gold "candles" and the big Christmas tree decorated along with a small one in one of the dormers.

December 22, 2002 – 4ᵗʰ Sunday of Advent
Wake Forest, N.C. – 8:25 p.m.
Sunny – 58 F

After going like a cyclone for the last two days, I had a vacation today – only four Masses and a baptism! Everything is relative. Actually, I was grateful for a day that went by so smoothly.

Before the 12:30 a.m. Mass, I talked with Tomás V., the member of the parish whose trailer house burned down on Monday. Fortunately, he, his wife and seven children, are all okay. I gave him a special blessing. He was teary, and I nearly was. We took up a second collection for him at the 12:30 p.m. Mass, and I announced the situation at all the Masses in English. I expect Tomás' family will receive more furniture and clothes and toys than they had before the fire!

Just before one of the Masses today, a man gave me a check for $500 to use for any emergency that might come up for the holidays. Naturally, I'm going to give it to Tomás' family, along with some other money from the parish and from donations.

One of the best photos I have ever taken was of Tomás' son Steven kneeling with a basketball, taken about a year ago.

Right before the 10:30 a.m. Mass, there was a crash at the entrance of the church. A young man named Kevin was making a U-turn to park in the street when he was hit by a non-parishioner's car. Though the other car hit Kevin's car on the driver's side, and although the car was probably totaled, Kevin was not hurt. In fact, he went right back to work. I'll check up on him tomorrow.

Dad called to see how the move went. Everything seems to be going fine in Ohio, and everyone is getting ready for the three days of non-stop Christmas celebrating.

This evening, as I was watching a fascinating movie, *Cross Creek*, I saw a group of candles coming down my driveway. I immediately guessed that they belonged to our Visions Youth Group, and I was right. Mark D. and the other adults came by with several teens to serenade me. I was honored to be the first house on their journey.

Now, I have to get ready for Christmas. Tomorrow will be a wonderful day at the office—because we really won't be working too hard. The biggest tasks I have to do tomorrow are to decorate the Christmas tree at church, do a little grocery shopping and practice my Spanish homily for Christmas. Naturally, I'll continue to decorate the house and get the beds made in the guest room, the master bedroom, and the art room (which is what I am calling the bonus room where I intend to get back into stained glass art and exercise).

December 23, 2002 – St. John Kanty
Wake Forest, N.C. – 8:45 p.m.
Sunny – 54 F

Miracle of miracles! The lights in the new parking lot are now in. The parking lot isn't paved yet, but we're closing in on it! The place looks wonderful with lamplight flooding a couple of acres of land. The new lights will definitely help with the Christmas Eve Masses because, for the most part, it will be dark when people are coming to church.

Today was a mellow day. Gael and I decorated the Christmas tree in the sanctuary, and we put up the new crèche that Mark Downing did. I can hardly wait for the kids to see the manger scene lit up. We put hay in it, and our figurines fit in perfectly. We have the crèche in front of the altar.

Though there are many things to unpack, and though I want to decorate the place, I'm going to take the rest of the evening off and watch a movie.

December 25, 2002 – Wednesday – Christmas
Wake Forest, N.C. – 8:10 p.m.
Partly sunny and very windy – 45 F

Yesterday morning, I received a call at the rectory from a man named George. He explained that he always likes to help those in need on Christmas Eve, but he had trouble this year coming up with someone to help as the Social Services office was closed. Did I know anyone who could use the help?

I told him about the Hispanic family with seven children whose house burned down a week ago. He made an appointment to bring some clothes for the family and some cash. In a half hour, he showed up with a box of clothes and $500 in cash. What a wonderful gesture. Others in the parish are also bringing the family clothes, money, sheets, furniture, towels, et cetera. In fact, there are so many donations that we have had to put someone in charge to coordinate the efforts.

Christmas Eve was, as usual, a zoo at St. Catherine's. The 4:00 p.m. Mass had between 800-900 people. Because it was rainy, and because the lower parking lot was muddy, I was surprised at how many came. The 6:00 p.m. Mass had around 700 people, while the 8:00 p.m. Mass in Spanish and the Midnight Mass had around 400 people each. This morning's 9:00 a.m. Mass had around 300 or so people. By the time I got home from the church this morning, I was very tired.

This Christmas finds me filled with gratitude and joy. I'm a priest and pastor. I'm very much needed by many people. The parish is growing rapidly and is extremely dynamic and Spirit-filled. I just moved into a beautiful new rectory. My health is good. I have great plans for writing in the coming year. And I have a wonderful family and friends. What more can a person ask for?

December 26, 2002 – Thursday, St. Stephen
Wake Forest, N.C. – 5:20 p.m.
Sunny – 45 F

It has been a very peaceful day. I got my study all decorated and the books put away. It's a beautiful place to do my work. Thanks be to God! Now all I have to do is be faithful in my writing.

My friend Arturo was over this morning with his mom. I drove them to RDU to catch a plane for Miami where they'll get one to Bogotá. Arturo's mom is not doing well. Arturo will be visiting in Colombia till January 16, when I'll be back at the airport to pick him up. While he's gone, I'll store his car in my garage.

One of the best Christmas gifts I received was from my brother, Larry and his wife, Sally. It is a wireless digital thermometer. You put a Thermo Sensor outdoors where it measures the temperature, and inside you have a unit indoors that shows you the temperature outside. I saw this at Mom and Dad's house and commented on how great it was. I'm eager to get it set up.

I also received a very interesting chalice and paten made from pottery. It's a little on the big side for me. I'm thinking of asking my friend Bill to go with me so I can exchange it at the store. My friend David has a set

I like, and perhaps I can get a set like that. Plus, I enjoy spending time with Bill.

December 28, 2002 – Saturday – Holy Innocents
Wake Forest, N.C. – 7:50 p.m.
Sunny – 50 F

This morning, I got to the church early to practice my Spanish homily and straighten up the place. Jesús came early, too and we spent some time together. He is doing such a fantastic job with the Hispanic youth ministry. St. Catherine's is very blessed to have him. I helped him load his truck with donated goods for Tomás' family. Unfortunately, the kids didn't show up, so it was only Jesús and Tomás who did all the work.

We had three baptisms today—two at 3:00 p.m. and one at the 5:00 p.m. Mass. Two of the babies were children of former teachers of St. Catherine's School.

Today at Mass, I talked about the duties of the "domestic church," the family that gathers at the table, in the living room and in the bedroom. I told the story of the father and teenage son who argued all the time. Finally, the dad took his son for a week camping trip to a mountain a couple hundred miles away. While on the mountain, they did lots of talking and had great adventures together. Their roles of rebellious son and domineering father began to fade away, and they discovered each other for what they were: Two human beings with different dreams, hopes, fears and loves. Instead of a mere camping trip, the adventure was a mountaintop experience. From that day forward, whenever they began to argue too strenuously, one or the other would merely say, "Remember the mountain."

I told the people how there are many fundamentalist preachers running around trying to make people believe that sinister forces are trying to destroy the family. Ridiculous! Nobody is trying to destroy the family. In fact, there is a greater variety of families now than ever before in human history! If there are problems in one's family, don't go looking around for a bogeyman to blame. Rather, look inside and fix it from within. The fundamentalist view of the world as intrinsically evil is diametrically opposed to the Catholic vision that sees the world as intrinsically good. After all, God created it.

Many people loved the homily and gave me positive strokes about it. I hope I touched a few hearts.

December 29, 2002 – Holy Family Sunday
Wake Forest, N.C. – 6:55 p.m.
Sunny – 50 F

Today was a beautiful day in many ways, sunny and warm. The Masses all went smoothly, and the people liked the homily. Whenever I speak on family and children, there is a great deal of enthusiasm. Perhaps that is because St. Catherine's is so much a young-family-oriented place. With 42 percent of our congregation 19 years old and younger, and with only 5 percent 60 and older, people are very interested in how to make their families stronger and holier.

One man came up to me after one of the Masses and asked about starting a new ministry. He would like to begin recording my homilies and making them available for those who are not able to come to Mass. They could also be available for people like him who travel a great deal. I asked him to see me to explore the idea. Others in the past have had that idea, but nobody has ever followed through. I think it could be a very worthwhile venture.

We gave out our St. Catherine calendars today, another annual ritual. This year, however, we had two choices: English and Spanish. The Spanish ones, especially, went like hotcakes.

The Hispanic community, as usual, made my day. We had a special surprise for Nayeli who was celebrating her 15th birthday. Not only did I offer the Mass for her (as well as for a relative of a parishioner who died on Christmas Day), but the Latino band also led the congregation in singing a special song for her after Mass.

After the Mass in Spanish, a woman came up to me and told me that she was probably going to join our parish. She is a native of Cleveland, my hometown, and has visited many churches. She likes the spirit of St. Catherine's. How could a person attend one of our Masses in Spanish and not get caught up in the Spirit-filled celebration with the awesome music and warm people?!

This evening, I received an email from a Methodist minister with whom I did my CPE (Clinical Pastoral Education) as a seminarian. He's pastor of a United Methodist Church in Siler City, N.C. I'm eager to hear how his life is unfolding.

I just finished watching a film on Padre Pio that a parishioner gave me. All through the film I was thinking of a man named George, who I believe has been thinking of becoming a Catholic. I think I'll call George tomorrow and let him know I was thinking of him throughout the film. Who knows? God speaks to us in all different ways, and via movies is just one way.

On the mission front, I'm trying to get Brad and Bill together so they can come up with some dates to get some missionary immersion experience in Mexico, Central America or South America. Perhaps this week will be the charm.

Meanwhile, the 10 people who are going to Honduras in March are selling chili to raise money for their trip. We plan on sending six teenagers and four adults. That will be our biggest mission group so far, and it will be the first with teenagers in the group.

December 30, 2002 – Tuesday
Wake Forest, N.C. – 8:55 p.m.
Sunny – 55 F

I talked with Mom and Dad last evening. Mom has a lump in one of her breasts in the same location that Jeanette had hers. The physicians did a biopsy, and now the waiting begins. This has put a cloud over the family's Christmas celebrations.

December 31, 2002 – Tuesday, New Year's Eve
Wake Forest, N.C. – 11:15 p.m.
Partly sunny – 67 F

I just received a phone call from Debbie L., a parishioner. She told me that one of our parish families was in an accident this evening on Capital

Blvd. Another car broadsided theirs, hitting them on the passenger side. Ginny was hurt and is now in surgery at WakeMed, and her husband, Ken is at the hospital. Their little son and daughter are fine. As soon as I write this note, I'll go to WakeMed to visit with Ken and assure him of my prayers. I will offer the Mass tomorrow for that family.

This last day of 2002 has been very warm, reaching 67 degrees. Men were working on our lower parking lot today, but I can't tell what they did. To me it looks like it did yesterday.

This year has been a very important one in my life and the life of the parish.

In the parish, the Trinity Center opened in August and, of course, the new rectory was completed this month. The lower parking lot is nearly completed, and the Diocese of Raleigh approved our parish's self-study in the spring. Our parish community continued to grow steadily, and the Hispanic community continued to become more and more organized. This year saw our first all-Spanish weekly bulletin, and this is the first year we have given out all-Spanish calendars along with English ones.

The one negative thing that happened to our parish this year was an upheaval in the school that saw many students leave. Shortly after the exodus, we accepted the resignation of the principal.

In my own life, this year has been mostly good. I have grown as a pastor, and my vision for the parish has become clearer. I am eager to begin the Full Stewardship program that I envision will pay off all our bills and build us a new sanctuary, office building and other structures. I am also eager to begin shooting the movie that I'll be in.

On the negative side of 2002, I have been attacked by a mentally unstable woman who is filled with rage and hate. She has enlisted the help of other right-wing hate-mongers. Fortunately, she has not gotten anywhere with the bishop or with the papal nuncio of the United States. She has a reputation for attacking priests and espousing pro-hate causes.

As this year comes to a close, I thank God for all the blessings that have been showered upon me and my parish. With God's help, next year will be even better!